JOE MADDY
of Interlochen

PROFILE OF A LEGEND

JOE MADDY
of Interlochen
PROFILE OF A LEGEND

NORMA LEE BROWNING

CB
CONTEMPORARY
BOOKS
CHICAGO

Library of Congress Cataloging-in-Publication Data

Browning, Norma Lee.
    Joe Maddy of Interlochen : profile of a legend / Norma Lee
Browning : foreword by W. Clement Stone : prologue by Van
Cliburn.
       p.   cm.
    ISBN 0-8092-3907-8 (cloth)
    1. Maddy, Joseph E. (Joseph Edgar), 1891–1966.   2. Music
teachers—United States—Biography.   3. National Music
Camp.   I. Title.
ML429.M18B8   1992
780′.92—dc20

                                              91-41124
[B]   CIP

Photos by Russell Ogg

Copyright © 1992 by Interlochen Center for the Arts
All rights reserved
Published by Contemporary Books, Inc.
180 North Michigan Avenue, Chicago, Illinois 60601
Manufactured in the United States of America
International Standard Book Number: 0-8092-3907-8

This book is dedicated to

Donna Stone, who shared her father's gift
for giving and enriched many lives,

Courtney Johnston, whose Uncle Russell shared
Dr. Maddy's dream and Mr. Stone's PMA,

and to

Everyone who has ever loved a child or felt the
magic of Interlochen.

CONTENTS

"If it had not been for W. Clement Stone, I am convinced that today Interlochen would be nothing more than a roadside plaque with the words 'This was once the site of the National Music Camp.' "

Don Currie
Chairman
Interlochen Board of Trustees

FOREWORD

In my book *The Success System That Never Fails*, I wrote a chapter on "The True Riches of Life."

In a subsection titled "The Fine Arts and the True Riches of Life," I wrote, "It was Norma Lee Browning who introduced me to one of the true riches of life—meeting and becoming a close personal friend of one of America's great men, Dr. Joseph E. Maddy."

I knew the first time I met him that here was a person I would like to have for a close friend. You don't have that feeling about very many people in a lifetime. But I knew instinctively from the moment he walked into our home that here was a good man. He was different. There was something about him that was very special.

Of course I've been a salesman all my life, and a good salesman can analyze people very quickly. Joe Maddy wasn't a salesman in the conventional sense. He wasn't out to make money for himself. He had already discovered the true riches of life. He was a salesman of dreams. I knew immediately that I wanted to help him, to be a part of his work, even if it cost money. I wanted to be a part of his life, to be permanently associated with him, to share in the dreams he had for these gifted young people.

Joe had already launched his National Music Camp and steered it through years of artistic acclaim beset by financial and other obstacles. His ultimate goal of turning his summer camp into a year-round arts center was turned down by his board of trustees.

He was warned repeatedly that he was going to "sink it."

I knew he wouldn't. I wouldn't let him.

That first meeting with Joe Maddy was on a warm evening in August 1961. Just thirty years ago. Today, the Interlochen Center for the Arts is recognized as one of the finest in the world. It is a splendid and shining monument to the man who had the dream and dug the holes.

We do not live in the past nor dwell on the past. But we must remember that the future is molded of mortar and bricks from the past, by men and women of noble character, ideals, and vision. Throughout history, the paths to greatness have been lit by noble ideas. Our Founding Fathers forged this great nation, the United States of America, with a nobility of words, ideas, and action in pursuit of liberty and human rights.

We have our founding fathers in other fields as well, in science, medicine, education, and the arts, and Joe Maddy was one of the giants among them. He had a special gift for inspiring and motivating others to achieve. He was a man of integrity, strength, and the courage to remain unshackled in his quest for a goal.

xii

Today, as we celebrate the hundredth anniversary of the birth of Interlochen's founder, we are awed by the magnitude of his "impossible" dream, by the magnificence of its fulfillment in physical reality.

But he did not do it alone. He could not. No one person single-handedly could build such an institution, an arts center that has become a citadel of freedom and beacon of hope for creative, gifted young people all over the world. Joe Maddy was the first to admit that he needed help, and he had many helpers along the way. I feel privileged and proud that I was one of them. It has been one of the true riches of my life.

Joe Maddy will always live in the hearts of everyone who knew him. For those who missed the opportunity to know him, he comes to life in this memoir. And for all of you my message is this: As we continue our never-ending search for new horizons of the future, we must never forget our great heritage of noble ideas from the past. We should treasure them and preserve them, and give thanks to our Creator for giving us this greatest of all gifts: Life with the heart and mind to dream dreams.

Joe Maddy's dream lives on. It is important to remember and cherish this man behind the magic of Interlochen.

W. Clement Stone
Winnetka, Illinois
August 1991

PREFACE

❧

In the beginning God created Interlochen.

Well, almost.

He had a couple of capable helpers, apostles Joe Maddy and Clem Stone.

Joe was helmsman of his own Noah's Ark, a fragile and flimsy thing crafted from a shoestring of gossamer dreams and loaded with a cargo of endangered species—young musical minstrels following the stars in search of a beachhead to call home.

There were starry-eyed violinists, cellists, tuba, bass, viola, and piccolo players—all doing their own thing from temple bells to bagpipes, and all enraptured by a dream: to make music together.

The Apostles' Creed, according to Joe Maddy, was "By Gum! We'll do it."

His musical Noah's Ark stayed afloat, barely, through years of stormy seas, with constant warnings from another species, called Bean Counters, that he was going to sink the thing.

Well, he didn't.

Just in the nick of time came Clem Stone to lend Joe a helping hand as First Mate and to bail him out of troubled waters with fiscal bait that left the Bean Counters boggle-eyed.

This book is an oral history of Interlochen from the beginning, told by those who have loved and cherished it. Interviews for this book were done from 1941 until Dr. Maddy's death on April 18, 1966; then in 1975 for the Retrospective and in August 1991 at the Joseph E. Maddy Centennial.

It is also a tribute to two great visionaries who have enriched our lives—and the world—with their dreams: Dr. Joe Maddy and Mr. W. Clement Stone.

In the writing of this book I will be charged with violating one of the basic tenets of the journalist's creed: objectivity. I plead guilty already: this book is unabashedly a "Hymn of Love" from the hearts of those who knew and worked with Joe Maddy.

I remember him in those "quiet times," the few precious stolen hours on a Monday afternoon, the camp's "day off," when he would sneak out to our house on the Boardman River and go trout fishing with my husband, and then the two of them would sit in the toolshed tying trout flies. These are the only times I can remember Dr. Maddy ever *sitting down*, and then he was always twitching his mustache and rubbing his bushy eyebrows, impatient to get back to camp.

From my many years of working with Dr. Maddy, numerous memories are clearly etched in my mind. But one stands out. During the taping of a show in his "Best of Interlochen" series, which aired on NBC radio and featured music and a guest speaker, the radio man told Dr. Maddy the program was running three minutes too long and asked tentatively, "Where should we cut the music?" Dr. Maddy replied without blinking an eye, "You can't cut the music. Just eliminate the speaker."

How can you be objective about a man like that?

Norma Lee Browning
Palm Springs, California
October 1991

ACKNOWLEDGMENTS

I am deeply grateful to W. Clement and Jessie V. Stone for making this book possible and thus bringing to fruition our own dream of perpetuating the memory of a man we loved.

I am deeply grateful to Linda E. Rupp who, as Mr. Stone's executive assistant, went far beyond the call of duty to help coordinate the project and propel it with her own editorial suggestions.

My special thanks to all of those at Interlochen who provided valuable assistance in many ways: President Dean Boal, LaVon Mattson, Margaret Henthorne, Roslyn Ridgway, Del Weliver; Don Currie, chairman of the Interlochen Board of Trustees; Don and Mary Gonzales, Gerald B. Fisher, Helen Osterlin, Dick Maddy, Wayne and Mary Brill, Dr. Joe and Ann Gadbaw, Jean Parsons, Dick Fiegel, and of course Peg and Melba, without whom this book couldn't have gone to press.

Special thanks also go to Courtney Johnston for transcribing the taped interviews, and to our assistants, Pat Burns and Pam Gallagher Hansen.

I owe a special debt of gratitude to Harvey Plotnick, publisher and president of Contemporary Books, Inc., for his encouragement, patience, and personal attention to expediting the creation of the completed book from the completed manuscript. Thanks also to Contemporary's managing editor, Kathy Willhoite, for shepherding the manuscript through the editorial process and to Contemporary's vigilant production editor, Cyndy Raucci.

JOE MADDY
of Interlochen
PROFILE OF A LEGEND

FAY MADDY: *The only reason he didn't sink it was—he didn't know when he was licked.*

JOE: *If I had known I was licked, it would have sunk a long time ago.*

BEAN COUNTER: *He runs it on intuition, not facts and figures. He's chasing butterflies.*

PART I
HE TOUCHED US
PERSONALLY

JOSEPH E. MADDY WAS ONE OF AMERICA'S pioneer music educators and founder of the world-famous National Music Camp at Interlochen, Michigan.

He started the camp in June 1928—with $15,000 of borrowed money, on fifty acres of land he didn't even own, and with only 115 students. Many of the students came to the camp on "scholarships," money from his own pocket, part of the small salary he earned as professor of music at the University of Michigan.

From its beginning the camp was a financial disaster. Its first season ended with a $40,000 debt, which rose to $67,000 the next year and $145,000 the next. But it won immediate and continuing critical acclaim from leading music educators and support from some of the great composers and conductors of the era: John Philip Sousa; Frederick Stock, conductor of the Chicago Symphony; Ossip Gabrilowitsch, conductor of the Detroit Symphony; Howard Hanson from the Eastman School of Music and Rochester (New York) Philharmonic; the Australian-born composer-conductor Percy Grainger; and, much later of course, the brilliant young concert pianist from Texas, Van Cliburn.

Most of these musicians, and many others as well, gave their time and services for benefit performances or as guest instructors for little or no fees. Their enthusiastic interest and participation helped spread the fame of the National Music Camp as the "world's foremost proving ground for youthful talent."

Meanwhile, Joe Maddy continued begging and borrowing money in pursuit of his ultimate dream of expanding the music camp into a year-round arts center. This goal was achieved with the opening of the Interlochen Arts Academy in September 1962. It was made possible through the generosity of Chicago multimillionaire philanthropist W. Clement Stone and his wife, Jessie V. Stone, who believed in Joe Maddy's dream enough to help make it come true.

Today, rather than a fifty-acre rustic camp, the Interlochen Center for the Arts is a modern, gleaming, scenic twelve-hundred-acre campus. It draws some two thousand students annually from every state and thirty-five foreign countries to the National Music Camp in summer for eight weeks of training in music, the visual arts, theater, and dance. Its students range from eight to eighteen years of age.

From September to June, the Interlochen Arts Academy operates as a private, coeducational boarding school for 430 high-school students, grades nine through twelve. There is equal emphasis on college-preparatory academics and the arts.

The Interlochen Center for the Arts is now completely debt-free, with built-up reserves and an established endowment fund. It is guided by a strong and vigilant board of trustees. It is located in the beautiful pinewoods-and-lakes country of northern Michigan, fifteen miles southwest of Traverse City, the state's "cherry capital."

1
PROLOGUE

Suddenly each summer on the lakeshores of northern Michigan a living truth is rekindled. I have felt its glow all the way around the world, across continents and across borderlines that only those who know a universal password can cross.

Interlochen is a magic word in the music world, and I felt its impact long before I became personally acquainted with it.

In the winter of 1961, while I was in Chicago making a recording, my mother telephoned me and said, "Now, Van, now don't get mad but I've already said yes to something I want you to do."

Dr. Joe Maddy had made a trip to Kilgore, Texas, to ask me to play a concert at his summer music camp at Interlochen. My mother is a very strong woman, not easily persuaded in matters relating to the advancement of my musical career. My mother and Dr. Maddy fell in love with each other, and from then on all I heard was, "Please, Van, I want you to do this for Dr. Maddy. I just have a good feeling about it." She has always had a sixth sense about things.

I had a concert tour scheduled. I couldn't interrupt it. I couldn't afford the time for a benefit performance at Interlochen. And frankly I was not enthralled with the idea of a summer camping trip.

I was even less enthralled when Dr. Maddy telephoned me to discuss the program just before camp opened. He wanted me to play the Tchaikovsky B-flat Minor Concerto, accompanied by a 180-piece high-school orchestra.

After recovering from the shock, I asked, "Did you say one hundred and eighty?" And *high-school* students?

"That's right," he said matter-of-factly.

"What about amplification—sound?" I asked, thinking of one piano amidst the din of nearly two hundred amateur musicians.

"Oh, don't worry about a thing," Dr. Maddy replied. "Everything will be all right."

And it was.

I never thought I would live to see the day when I would play a concert in corduroys and shirtsleeves. The outdoor Interlochen stage is the only place I have ever performed without full formal concert attire. But formal concert dress could not have made the performance more dignified, for it already had achieved its own dignity in the inspired musicianship of these youngsters in blue knickers.

We played the Tchaikovsky that first summer and the Rachmaninoff Third Piano Concerto the next summer, 1962, with only one week of rehearsals.

If I live to be ninety I will never forget it. I doubt that any other high-school orchestra has performed the Third Rachmaninoff.

6

So my mother turned out to be right, as usual, and I owe her a special debt of gratitude for introducing me to Dr. Maddy and Interlochen. Her birth date is the same as Dr. Maddy's, October 14. This year, 1991, is Dr. Maddy's centennial and my mother's ninety-fifth.

Dr. Maddy's life reflected the hope, vigor, and individualism of the American spirit. His dream projected a vision of youth at its best, framed in the moral and artistic guidelines of individual, competitive freedom. Too much of this has vanished from the American scene.

The world changes. We are now computerized. But music comes from the soul, not a computer. Interlochen remains a beacon too precious and too fragile to lose in the fog of futuristic computerizing. America should be proud and grateful for this vital training ground where our nation's youth learns not only music but universal values.

Interlochen was one of the most thrilling experiences of my life. My heart is still so much there, as is my allegiance. We should cherish these young people who can look you straight in the eye and play straight from the heart. My mother and I take great pride and pleasure, as we all should, in saluting this man, Dr. Joseph Maddy, whose dreams and pioneering spirit kept the thread of music and youth fastened to the stars. And we give a special salute to W. Clement Stone and his dear wife, Jessie, who helped him so generously.

Van Cliburn
Fort Worth, Texas
September 1991

7

2
I REMEMBER

🌿

I remember well the first time I met Joe Maddy. How could I forget it? When Clement told me that Norma Lee and Russell were bringing this wonderful man over for dinner on a Sunday, and he had invited some other people, too, I almost panicked.

Our maid had just quit without notice and I had not cooked for a very long time. I went to church that morning and after the service I told our minister about my predicament and how nervous I was about cooking for all these people, especially for this man Dr. Maddy because I had never met him.

I asked, "What should I do?"

He said, "Just roll up your sleeves and get to work."

So I did. I don't remember what I cooked and probably neither does anyone else. They were all simply mesmerized by this man Dr. Maddy—and so was I. He started talking and telling us about this place called Interlochen. He was so dedicated to it, and there was so much love in his heart and in his eyes. He talked softly but with real passion about this place and his kids who came there. There was a sweetness and gentleness about him.

We had never been to Interlochen, but this man so impressed me that I was perfectly willing to do anything I could to help him.

Jessie V. Stone
Winnetka, Illinois
August 1991

3
To Joe with Love

"Joe's outstanding quality was love. He was capable of a lot of that. He loved this camp and the kids more than anything. He would always say, 'They don't know they can't, so they do.' I heard him say that lots of times. He was like that, too. The kids learned it from him."

❧

I first met him when I was fifteen. He was seventeen. We played in the Sunday school orchestra in the Christian Church in Wellington, Kansas. I played flute and he played the violin. I had taken only thirteen lessons. He used to tell me I couldn't play on that old flute. I wasn't the greatest flute player in the world, but I learned to play the piccolo solo part in "The Stars and Stripes Forever." Joe liked that.

Whenever Joe wanted anything, he tried until he got it. Tenacity was one of his traits. So was sincerity. He didn't believe one thing and let on another. He also had integrity. He was honest about what he wanted. He never wasted time. He'd get up early. He was available. He never felt so important that people wouldn't bother him. They would telephone him at any hour of the night and he was always at their service.

There were hardships at Interlochen, but that was the happiest time of my life. I couldn't keep up with his traveling. It was hard to juggle everything. I liked staying at home. I enjoyed everyone around me. He loved playing quartets, and I always stayed up and listened to them.

I think I was so in love with him that anything he wanted to do was okay with me. That's the way it was.

I never played or taught there. But sometimes I would practice with the orchestra, just for fun. The kids were so invigorating and enthusiastic about what they were doing. That's why Joe would always say, "They don't know they can't, so they do."

He also always said, "The difficult is easy. The impossible takes a little longer, a little more work."

After he got Van Cliburn to come here for benefit concerts, he was always on the phone trying to reach Van at one place or another. Once I laughed and asked him if he had ever stopped to think that he didn't own Van Cliburn.

He said, "If we don't own Van Cliburn, who does?"

I told this to Van, and Van said, "He is absolutely right, and don't you ever forget it."

You couldn't stop him. You couldn't slow him down. One time in Chicago, driving at ninety miles an hour in heavy traffic, we hit ice and the car skidded and turned around and around. We didn't hit anyone. We've had many narrow escapes. Ninety miles an hour was his gait. It didn't do any good to tell him to slow down.

That's the way he was in everything he did.

Except fishing. He was so tense most of the time, but when he was wading in those trout streams he was absolutely relaxed. I went fishing with him a lot in the rivers around Interlochen. But the ocean—it was too violent.

Joe loved deep-sea fishing. We took our trailer to Marathon, Florida, each year when we could afford it so Joe could go deep-sea fishing. Sometimes Mr. and Mrs. Stone

11

would fly down and join us. The first time I went out with them was not so good. The scenery was great, but the boat made me deathly ill. They didn't ask me to go anymore.

Once Joe went out with a friend early in the morning and said he would be back by four o'clock in the afternoon. His friend came at three o'clock and said he hadn't seen Joe for over an hour. He said a storm had come up and waves over ten feet high had knocked Joe out of his boat. It was just a little outboard motorboat. It went around in circles and finally came back to where Joe was paddling in the water with sharks all around him. He crawled into the boat and got to shore. Everyone in our trailer park thought it was absolutely wonderful, a miracle. Here was the man who fell in the ocean and survived.

Joe said, "Don't scold me. It happened for a reason. I know God saved me because I have some unfinished work to do."

I never doubted him. He was always up, never down. There was only one time at Interlochen, when we were sitting there in our trailer and watching the lake, and he was very, very low . . .

I said, "Joe, let's pray."

He said, "What do you think I've been doing all this time?"

But he never stayed down very long.

Fay Maddy
Prescott, Arizona
1970

4
MY MAGNIFICENT OBSESSION

"What the mind of man can conceive and believe, the mind of man can achieve."

❧

That has always been my philosophy. It was Joe Maddy's philosophy, too. He had a dream. He had faith. He had courage. But more important, he had determination to achieve his goals.

The key to success is repetition, repetition, repetition. It's the old Horatio Alger formula: If at first you don't succeed, try again.

I learned this very early in life. I was six years old, selling newspapers on Chicago's tough South Side, and it wasn't easy. I was scared. There was a place, Hoelle's Restaurant, near the corner where I tried to work. From the outside it looked like a busy and prosperous place but was frightening to a six-year-old child who had never been inside a restaurant. I decided to give it a try. I was nervous, but I walked in hurriedly and made a lucky sale at the first table. Then diners at the second and third tables bought papers. When I started for the fourth table, Mr. Hoelle pushed me out the front door.

But I had sold three papers. So when Mr. Hoelle wasn't looking, I walked back in and called at the fourth table. Apparently, the jovial customer liked my gumption; he had paid for the paper and given me an extra dime before Mr. Hoelle pushed me out again. But I had already sold four papers and got a "bonus" dime besides. I walked into the restaurant and started selling again. There was a lot of laughter. The customers were enjoying the show. One whispered loudly, "Let him be," as Mr. Hoelle came toward me. About five minutes later, I had sold all my papers.

The next evening I went back. Mr. Hoelle again ushered me out the front door. But when I walked right back in, he threw his hands in the air and exclaimed, "What's the use!" Later, we became great friends and I never had trouble selling papers there again.

Years later, I used to think of that little boy, almost as if he were not me but some strange friend from long ago. Once, after I had made my fortune and was head of a large insurance empire, I analyzed that boy's actions in the light of what I had learned. This is what I concluded:

1. He needed the money. The newspapers would be worthless to him if they weren't sold; he couldn't even read them. The few pennies he had borrowed to buy them would also be lost. To a six-year-old, this catastrophe was enough to motivate him—to make him keep trying. Thus he had the necessary *inspiration to action.*

2. After his first success at selling three papers in the restaurant, he went back in, even though he knew that he might be embarrassed and thrown out again. After three trips in and out, he had the necessary technique for selling newspapers in restaurants. Thus, he gained the *know-how.*

3. He knew what to say because he had heard the older kids yelling out the headlines. All he had to do, when he approached a prospective customer, was to repeat in a softer voice what he had heard. Thus, he possessed the requisite *activity knowledge.*

I realized that my "little friend" had become successful as a newsboy by using the same techniques that later flowered into a system for success that enabled him, and others, to amass fortunes. The keys are motivation, know-how, and action.

I have told this story in my book *The Success System That Never Fails,* and I have retold it many times and will continue to do so. I believe it illustrates the importance of something as applicable today as it was then, that we can achieve anything we want if we believe in it and work and try hard enough.

Joe Maddy was the embodiment of this philosophy.

Though we never discussed it, our lives were parallel in many ways. He was a very motivated person. But he was motivated by a dream. I was motivated by money—from necessity.

After I acquired wealth, I was motivated by a "magnificent obsession" to share it with others. The book *Magnificent Obsession* by Lloyd C. Douglas had a great influence on my life. I learned and believed—and still do—that anything you give to others comes back to you tenfold and more.

Joe Maddy's "magnificent obsession" was Interlochen. The riches he reaped from it can't be measured in monetary terms. Many persons have asked why Jessie and I have given so much to Interlochen. Yes, the first time we met at our home, I observed that his shoes were shined and polished, his suit well pressed, his handshake firm and strong. But there was something more—the look in his eyes. I knew he was a *good* man, and I wanted to be a part of his life and really help him.

Money is only good for the good it can do to help others, and it never occurred to me that I wouldn't always have money. I always knew that there was nothing in life I couldn't have if I really wanted it and paid the price for it—in an honorable fashion. I had a strong religious background and training. I think the good Lord really wants to help those people who are trying to make this world a better place to live in, and Joe Maddy was one of them.

Many years ago I made a resolution that through the grace of God I'd do everything to make this world a better place to live in, for this and future generations.

I have tried to achieve this goal. I believe I have done it partly through sharing what I have with others. I look on my financial contributions as payment for the privilege of giving.

Joe Maddy was a giver in the finest sense. He gave his life to an "impossible dream" that no one else believed in but Joe Maddy. After I met him, I believed in it, too, because I believed in Joe Maddy.

I felt he was a man of character and was devoting his life to a cause he believed in. He had the faith, the courage, the motivation and inspiration, the goals and plans, everything he needed for this great achievement. The only thing he needed and didn't have apparently was financial help. It has always been a part of my philosophy that one of the greatest joys in the world is to be a part of a great person's life, particularly when that person is influencing so many lives. And what a wonderful feeling it is to know that merely by signing a check you become part of it.

When you stop to consider that very often a person does so much and gets so little for influencing the lives of others, it makes you want to be the catalyst in seeing to it that he can carry on his life's work. Joe Maddy always had to struggle to keep the camp going. Then his board turned down his dream of an academy. It seemed to me it would be easy to become a part of his life by supplying something he could not supply himself, and that was the necessary funding to get the Academy started.

So I accepted his invitation to be on the board of trustees, because I knew he needed my help so he could influence the other trustees.

Jessie and I both had great admiration for Dr. Maddy and Fay. We became very friendly. We always enjoyed our visits to Interlochen. Of course I had to be there for board meetings, but we went anyway between board meetings when we had the opportunity.

We often flew down to Florida to join the Maddys for three days of deep-sea fishing. Those were interesting experiences. Before we met, I wouldn't have dreamed of going down to Florida to vacation for three days, and we had never been deep-sea fishing. But it was very healthful, we met some very interesting people, and we developed an interest in a sport that we came to like. In fact, we became very successful at it, both Jessie and I. But especially Jessie.

At Interlochen, we developed a greater appreciation for the arts than we had had before. I still probably can't name

17

more than half a dozen operas that I would recognize, but it was always thrilling to watch the young people perform, no matter what they were performing.

My blessings are far beyond anything I could ever expect to earn. I thank God for these blessings. Among the best of them was the privilege of knowing and helping Joe Maddy.

W. Clement Stone
Winnetka, Illinois
August 1991

GEORGE MACKMILLER: *Joe Maddy doesn't believe in having money in the bank. He spends tomorrow's money yesterday.*

CLEM: *Well, I've done that myself.*

JOE: *Mack is a dedicated man, but he's a bookkeeper. He worries too much about details.*

PART II
THE DREAMERS
AND THE BEAN
COUNTERS

THERE'S THE MAN WHO DREAMS the dreams and the man who counts the beans. That's one lesson I've learned from working with Mr. Stone. I think that's why he and Dr. Maddy hit it off so well. They were the men who dreamed the dreams and let the bean counters worry about where the money comes from.

I remember times when bills were coming due and the cash flow was slow, and our accountant Ken Danielson would say, "Mr. Stone, you can't spend any more money. You can't give any more money away. Don't pledge any more money, don't spend anything, because we don't have the money."

And Mr. Stone would say, "Ken, that's your problem, not mine. I have these things I need to do, I need to make

21

these gifts, and you need to find the money to pay for them. But it's your problem, not mine."

All dreamers of dreams have their bean counters.

Linda E. Rupp
Executive Assistant to W. Clement Stone
Lake Forest, Illinois
September 1991

5
JOE MADDY, DREAMER

❧

- He had a little-boy smile and the guts of a Comanche.

- He loved digging holes in the ground, and, like his dreams, the holes had no definite dimensions. If the bills went unpaid, he took the transcendental approach. Let the bean counters worry.

- He ran his camp by serendipity and brought snap, crackle, and spark to music pedagogy. He touched more lives, shaped more careers, and entered far more hearts than any other music educator.

- He lived for only one thing—helping young people make music together. He guided his kids with bold and loving strokes. When they hit a sour note, he said, "Don't worry. You'll do better next time."

- When a bassoon player's key stuck during a concert, he tricked the audience into giving him time to fix it. When he bought his first harp but had no one to play it, he quickly taught a young pianist how to push the pedals and pluck the strings for a one-chord cadenza. When he needed an aquaplane for a waterfront show, he invented one.

• He never walked adagio, always presto or allegro. He walked and talked fast. He drove dangerously, and once nearly crash-landed a small plane on Kresge Auditorium.

• He was imbued with the resilience of Kansas wheat fields, the endurance of the granite hills of Vermont, and a Missouri-mule bullheadedness that refused to recognize the impossible.

• He had a mind as quick as lightning and a wisdom of the heart. He had a compassion for his fellow humans and a passionate devotion to the highest ideals of the human spirit.

• He embodied values, such as the work ethic this country was founded on. He wanted to make the world a better place to live in. He was always bursting forth with ideas. No one could stop him.

• He was sui generis, one of a kind, an original.

Not everyone was rhapsodic about Joe Maddy. There were the dissidents.

But this is the way I remember him. The years have come and gone. The memories remain, etched in my heart forever.

It was a balmy summer night in August 1941 when I got hooked on Interlochen. Fifty years ago, almost to the day. My husband, Russell Ogg, and I were newlyweds. On an assignment in northern Michigan, I saw a sign that said National Music Camp. I said, "We've got to go there. I want to see if it's what I always dreamed it would be."

My childhood dream was to go to Interlochen. But I played only tenor sax, and there was no earthshaking need for a saxophone in the music camp orchestra. I couldn't qualify for a scholarship. Besides, my music teacher gently told me that I could write poetry better than I could play the saxophone and advised me to go into journalism. So I traded my saxophone for a typewriter.

We walked down to the Interlochen Bowl that night, just as Howard Hanson began conducting the orchestra in his *Romantic Symphony*. It changed our lives.

In our photojournalism jobs we covered many assign-ments all over the world, but between the fires and murders and other trivia of our trade, we always managed to get home to Interlochen. "Home" was H-1, an ancient and creaky two-story house of quaint and bucolic charm. It was called H-1 for a simple and logical reason: It was the first house on Faculty Row. It had two bathrooms for twelve people, one upstairs, one downstairs.

The first time we moved in, I took a fast look around and said, "Hmmmmmmm."

Russell said cheerfully, "Well, honey, it's not the Palmer House."

We adjusted. We grew very fond of H-1 and looked forward eagerly to each summer's sojourns there. H-1 on Faculty Row was a prestigious address by primitive, north-woods standards because it had a front porch and a com-manding view of the narrow dirt road that people like

Percy Grainger trotted up and down in his shorts and knee socks.

And across the road, T. P. Giddings with the goatee would be wiggling his finger at someone, which meant, "Come play chess with me." This was only on those rare occasions when he wasn't talking oscilloscopes or tying someone to a tree for disciplinary problems.

Our front porch at H-1 was the epicenter of the cacophony of Interlochen. We were enshrined with the constant blare of trumpets, trombones, and bass tubas, the screeching of violins, and the sound of would-be opera singers in their practice cubicles or on tree stumps. Everywhere. It was never ending.

The other occupants of H-1 were VIP faculty and staff and a few bats. We were neither faculty nor staff yet. Except for George Mackmiller, the bookkeeper, we were the only nonmusicians in camp. Our housemates were all people with impressive credentials: Maynard Klein, the beloved choral director, and his wife, Isla; Sig Swanson, the trombone teacher; Hildegarde Lewis, the dance director; Dr. Maddy's chiefs of staff Peg Stace, Melba Bram, and Mary Frances James; and others. I'm sure they wondered at first what we were doing in H-1 on Faculty Row, a couple of itinerant, nonmusical mavericks with cameras and a typewriter.

We were there because that's where Joe Maddy put us. I always suspected he did it so Peg and Melba, his chief vigilantes, could keep an eye on us, and scrutinize us. Could we really belong or not?

We tried. Russell spent most of his spare time in the Shed with the maintenance crew. He was handy with tools. He always fixed the plumbing and took care of the bats.

26

Eventually, we both succumbed to the spirit of the place. He started taking cello lessons. I struggled through beginner's piano lessons, but my repertoire never got beyond "Glow Worm" and "Little Red Wing." I did better on the guitar, which I had learned to play at Chicago's Old Town School of Folk Music as part of a newspaper assignment.

In those days, folk music wasn't on the Interlochen agenda, but I once sneaked my guitar out to camp and gave a private concert for our compatriots in H-1. They were obviously amused but constrained in their accolades. No one invited me to audition for concertos or to come to Bloody Friday tryouts.

Naturally I did not invite Dr. Maddy. But he caught me in the act years later when he crashed a party at our house on the Boardman River. We had a weekend guest from Chicago, a friend from the Old Town School of Folk Music. She played banjo. We billed ourselves as the Sunshine Sisters and played duets frequently for an enthralled audience of two—us!

We were sitting cross-legged on the floor, totally enraptured with our own renditions of "Red River Valley" and "On Top of Old Smokey" when, suddenly, unexpectedly, Dr. Maddy walked in.

He wasn't alone. He had two distinguished guests with him—Mr. W. Clement Stone *and* Van Cliburn.

It's a good thing we were already sitting down.

Van Cliburn nearly cracked up. Our paths have crossed many times through the years. He always greets me with a big hug and kiss, a wide grin, and the same words: "I'll never forget that night on the Boardman when you played the guitar for me."

What we lacked in musical talent we tried to make up

for in other ways. But I think the bona fide seal of approval of our occupancy in H-1 really came when we parked my antique London barrel organ on the front porch. I had bought it at an auction barn somewhere in rural Iowa while on a city-girl-in-the-country assignment. It was lovely, loud, and added to the general cacophony along Faculty Row. It also stopped a lot of people in their tracks on that dirt road.

In the early days of Interlochen, everyone worked long, hard hours, but no one worked for the money. Salaries, if any, were minimal. Ours? Room and board and half of what we made from selling Russell's pictures. Ho ho. He couldn't sell; he gave them away. But we both had newspaper jobs and big-hearted editors who put on their blinders and gave us extra vacation time to spend at Interlochen. They also used all the pictures and stories we sent them.

And Russell turned out glorious pictures in his very makeshift photo lab. The camp's physical facilities were almost as bleak as its fiscal structure.

One day Dr. Maddy came to Russell and said, "I want this picture blown up. Big. Like a mural. I'm going to hang it on the wall in the hotel."

Russell said, "Dr. Maddy, we can't do that. Even if I could blow it up to the size you want, there's no place to wash the print. We can't build a print-wash tank that big."

Dr. Maddy snapped, "There's the lake, isn't there? It's got lots of water in it."

No one ever knew how the print was made, but one night after taps, while the rest of the camp slept, everyone from H-1 trekked down to the waterfront with flashlights to watch Russell and Maynard, the choral director, gingerly washing that big mural in the lake. It was a picture of the orchestra in the Interlochen Bowl with Dr. Maddy conducting and Hildegarde's dancers on the roof. It still hangs today, in the lobby of the Joe Maddy Administration Building.

Faculty Row has changed. The dirt road is paved now and lined with twentieth-century upscale scholarship lodges that have names instead of numbers, names like Brahms and Beethoven, and even street signs—such as Percy Grainger Lane.

Joe Maddy was the perennial Peter Pan–Pied Piper of dreams and make-believe. He knew that if you believed it enough, it would happen. And it did. For me, it was an awesome, Alice-in-Wonderland adventure into an unknown world of music and magic. I'm glad I was there.

6
JOE'S CEREBRAL SIDEKICK—
T.P.

*"The third day I saw him, I looked at him and said,
'There's brains behind those eyes.' "*

T.P.

❦

Joe Maddy and T. P. Giddings lived at the same boarding-house in Chautauqua Lake, New York, and when they met it was instant cerebral rapport, a fortuitous meeting of minds.

At Interlochen, T.P. was known as the colorful, goa-teed, straitlaced Disciplinarian, with a capital D, who could shush anything or anybody with a fearful wiggle of his forefinger.

But he was much more than that. He was Joe Maddy's amanuensis, mentor, and soulmate in nonconformity. They were strikingly different in physical appearance and action. Dr. Maddy was perpetual motion; T.P. was slow motion. But they were intellectual twins in their rebellion against the established rules of academia. Both fervently believed in academic freedom to do things their own way, though each had reached this pinnacle of self-confidence indepen-dently.

Dr. Maddy always liked to tell people, "Not being

educated, I don't have to quote anybody or follow anybody's lead."

But he quoted T.P. liberally in his Sunday Sermons on
the Mount and faithfully followed the rules he learned from
him. Together they made a great team in the shaping up of
Interlochen.

GEMS FROM INTERVIEWS WITH T.P. IN THE 1940S AND 1950S

I don't know which end of the string bass you put in your
mouth, but I know how to make people behave. I did the
dirty work for Joe Maddy.

I was up-and-coming, always ready to do things. No
one was a better do-thinger than I was. In my childhood, it
was not music that attracted me but the chance to show off
that drove me to toil. I was not quite twelve when I began
to play the church organ. My mother once said, "You played
very nicely, Thaddy, but it was very apparent who enjoyed
your playing the most." (His real name was Thaddeus but
most people called him T.P.)

I went to a country school but my mother was very
ambitious for me. She would buy books for the next grade
ahead of me. So I did six grades in three and a half years.

I was one of the smartest men who ever went to the
University of Minnesota. It took me only eight months to
get a request never to return.

I worked in a starch factory for one year, then became
superintendent of schools in Anoka County, Minnesota.
The faculty was me and a girl in a two-room schoolhouse.
I took music lessons for a dollar an hour, and that was my
education in public school music. Then I became supervi-

sor of music in Minneapolis and taught at the University of Minnesota for fourteen years. When people ask, "Where did you study?," I say I never studied.

The things you need to learn aren't taught in school. Those that have any sense to them you already know.

The normal school today is a late invention of the devil. Most universities are not practical. You put four years into an education and most of it is trash. The teachers have to fill it up with something. If you're going to teach music in schools, you need to know how to run a class. Every kid has to be taught that learning is hard work, whether the subject is music or mathematics or reading. Teachers are always trying to find some easy way. There isn't any.

Get them interested in hard work and you've solved the educational problem. There is nothing worthwhile that isn't hard work.

REMEMBERING T.P.

The remainder of this chapter consists of excerpts from interviews conducted in 1975.

KEN JEWELL

My wife, Mary, and I were walking around the camp one day, and along came this man with a funny little Vandyke goatee. He wiggled his finger at us, pointed to a nearby bench and said, "Hey, you two, sit down. I'm going to sing you a song. This is the symphony that Schubert wrote and never finished." Then he began to sing to us. When he finished, he said, "I'm T. P. Giddings. There now, you'll never forget me. Good-bye." And he was gone. We later

32

became better acquainted. I played chess with him a lot. He was a marvelous man.

FRED FENNELL

You could search the world over and never find two men more perfect for each other than T.P. and Joe. T.P. had eyes in the back of his head, and the side of his head, too. You were never quite sure when he would show up at a rehearsal. He never interfered, he just listened, and then you never knew who he was listening to. Sometimes he was behind the stage or off to the side. Sometimes he would see a kid slouched in his chair. The kid never slouched again after T.P. finished with him. Slouching was not only bad posture, but a slouching kid couldn't breathe right. I learned to breathe from T.P. Every kid in camp learned to breathe from him. He would say, "Boy, stand up straight. You're not breathing right." Once they learned to breathe right, he would go and buy them an ice-cream cone.

Once he tied me to a tree because he thought I was too active. He whipped out a rope and said, "Boy, I'm going to teach you a lesson. I just want you to stand there for a while and think what a beautiful day this is, and that you don't have to be quite that busy and all over the place." He stood there staring at me in stony-faced silence for a few minutes. Then he said, "All right, boy," and untied me.

He had a knack for picking out the kids who would be troublemakers. His eyes were always on you, but there was the charm of that wonderful smile underneath. He usually wore a straw hat and looked like he didn't know enough to come in out of the rain. But he was a great disciplinarian. Joe didn't need to worry about disciplining anybody; that was T.P.'s job. He was a master at it. He didn't beat around the bush.

Both Joe and T.P. were interested in bringing more music to more kids—not in gleaning every note to perfection, but in awakening sounds in their ears and excitement in their minds and bodies.

BILL REVELLI

Joe and T.P. made a great team, like Rodgers and Hammerstein. T.P. was uncompromising and pretty straitlaced about things. Kids sometimes looked at him as an old fogey, but they also liked him in their own way. They had tremendous respect for him. He watched over those kids like a mother hen.

A. CLYDE ROLLER

He used to joke with the conductors by saying, "Those who can't teach, conduct." He was the camp's first ecologist. Whenever anybody broke a twig off a tree he would get very upset. He didn't believe in messing around with Mother Nature.

MARCIA WEISSGERBER PALMER

As a youngster I was absolutely petrified of him. He was always "shushing" people. Whenever he would stand near my chair, I would just shake all over for fear he would shush me. I couldn't move the bow on the strings.

Of course when I knew him later, I wasn't so afraid of him. He was a dear, sweet, fabulous person. He had a lot of foresight, and I suppose that without his support Joe Maddy would have made the camp work some other way but he was a tremendous help in the making of Interlochen.

ORIEN DALLEY

We had this terrific bassoonist who developed a walking problem. During rehearsals we noticed that his balance was a little off when walking to his chair. He gradually got worse. The doctors said nothing was wrong with him, but he began showing up late to rehearsals and sometimes missing them altogether. One day he came wobbling to the Bowl with the aid of a cane.

T.P. grabbed the cane from him and drew a line in the dirt twenty feet long. He said, "Bill, you walk down that line, and if you miss the line one step, you are going to be sent home and to the nuthouse." Bill straightened up, walked the line, and there was no more trouble.

GEORGE WILSON

I was a young teacher, fresh out of college, and new to Interlochen. Dr. Maddy told me many times that T.P. was the educator and he—Maddy—was the idea man and musician. He told me I should watch and listen to T.P. because I could learn about teaching from him.

Well, I learned a lot about teaching from T.P. Some of it was good, some not so good. But I owe him a lot. He was always welcome at my rehearsals, but he was not always welcome at rehearsals of other conductors.

He would sit in on the rehearsals quietly. We called him Stony Face. He never cracked a smile. But if you made any move, any little noise from the scraping of a chair or an instrument, or the crunching of your feet in the sand on the stage—and there was always sand on the stage—he would wiggle his finger, which meant trouble.

There is no way to describe it, how he wiggled that finger, and he did it to everyone—faculty, staff, students, guests. He never stopped. He worked on everyone.

When rehearsal was over, he would look you straight in the eye and wiggle his finger again, this time with an ominous come-hither sign that meant, "Now you are going to get a lesson on what you've done wrong."

When he wiggled his finger at me, I usually knew what to expect. It always went something like this:

"Young man, do you know what you did wrong?"

"No."

"Do you know how many times you gave your students directions, how many times you told them to do something? The same thing?"

"No."

"Four times you told them, and once is enough."

T.P. was never inhibited about giving conductors conducting lessons, though he knew nothing about conducting. He derived great pleasure in telling people that what they were doing was wrong. As a young teacher suddenly conducting string orchestra and band at Interlochen, I listened carefully to T.P. And I was learning.

7
JOE'S SERMONS ON THE MOUNT

"If you don't like the rules, get out and stay out."

꽃

Few men in the history of music education have earned more voluble and endearing epithets than Joe Maddy. He was frequently characterized as a "reckless rebel," a "wholesome fanatic," a "benevolent despot," and a "damn fool."

It bothered him not a whit.

Many of these intonations were invoked by his mania for digging holes and his passion for expounding on what he was going to do with them at his Sunday morning "Sermons on the Mount," as some people called them.

He had a habit of mixing metaphors, music, and a lot of vital statistics on everything from communism to world peace. He would quote from Matthew, Mark, Luke, and Brahms, and his own Fourteen Steps to Musicianship, as a spinoff to the values and virtues of free enterprise and the work ethic, and the evils of government bureaucracy, the

New Deal, Petrilloism,* cultural illiteracy, and especially the public school system.

In the opinion of many, Joe Maddy's weekly message wasn't a religious sermon, it was a political sermon. Rather irreverent.

But he was not irreligious. He was well read in religious books and philosophy, was a very moral person who demanded high standards from others, and was a firm believer in religious freedom.

To him, freedom of religion implied freedom *from* religion as well. And freedom of speech—the freedom to speak out on the things he believed in.

No one was *required* to go to Interlochen's Sunday services. Students were free to go into town to the church of their choice. A camp bus would take them.

Even T.P. wouldn't dare wiggle his finger at anyone to make them sit through Joe Maddy's sermons.

Dr. Maddy wasn't the greatest speaker in the world. He was often inarticulate and fumbling, and he talked too fast. But he had a boyishly compelling presence on stage as he talked rapturously about the wonders of Interlochen and the agonies of trying to remake the world in its image.

---

*James C. Petrillo was president of the Chicago Federation of Musicians and widely known as the Czar of Music. In the early 1940s, he banned all broadcasts from Interlochen because they were performed by students, nonunion musicians. He also banned all union members from teaching at Interlochen. Dr. Maddy's long fight with the powerful union leader made national headlines and is recorded in the 1963 book *Joe Maddy of Interlochen* by Norma Lee Browning. Also see Chapter 27 of this book.

People sometimes sat in puzzlement and wonder at the audacity of this man's astronomical flights of fancy. They might not comprehend all the words, but they got the message.

Through the years, from the early 1940s until Joe Maddy's death on Monday, April 18, 1966, I sat through many of his "Sermons on the Mount," utterly spellbound and fascinated. As a journalist I also took copious notes in shorthand notebooks that are now withered and worn and replaced by word processors and computers. Computers can never recapture what went on in Joe Maddy's mind. But my notebooks did. Old age has faded them, but they are still legible.

Here are some gems from the crown jewels of rhetoric at Joe Maddy's Sunday Sermons on the Mount. Quoted verbatim.

EXCERPTS FROM SERMONS ON THE MOUNT

We've been so busy fighting the Indians that we have become a nation of cultural illiterates. We first had to conquer the Indians and then conquer the world, and we have nothing to show for it but material things. Our government is spending ten thousand times as much toward war than toward peace.

The public schools are not doing their job.

There's no chance to develop a Heifetz in this country because the schools won't give kids time to practice. In most high schools there are forty-two athletic teachers to every one music teacher. We have subdued the Indians; now we must develop our human resources. We have made a little progress. This has not been because of the schools but in spite of them.

What more can we expect to do in this world than to leave it a little bit better? There is more compensation in making people happier than in making all the money in the world. But it's hard work. All the great composers— Brahms, Bach, Beethoven, Mozart—all of them had to work hard, but they were also divinely inspired. No person can do great inspirational, creative work until he is divinely inspired. Handel composed the *Messiah* in twenty-one days. Now let's look at Interlochen.

When Howard Hanson took his orchestra on a tour to Europe, there were more than forty Interlochen students in his seventy-piece orchestra. They got encores everywhere they went, but when they ended in Russia and played "The Stars and Stripes Forever," they got eight standing ovations. The people chanted, "We like Americans because Americans like God." Now isn't that peculiar for a communist country?

Today we're spending $48 billion for military preparations when all we need is more musical missionaries for peace in this world.

So people call me a damn fool and a rebel. Yes, I'm a rebel against the traditions that prevent the growth of character in our students. We have strict rules. If you don't like the rules, I say get out and stay out. If you want to play baseball, this isn't the place to come. You could hit a finger and not be able to play piano or fiddle. If a kid is too good a harpist for a bad teacher, I get rid of the teacher.

This is the greatest assemblage of musical talent in the world, and you cannot mix music with cruelty. Musicians are kind people. They're interested in beauty and harmony in this world. But they are limited because our educational system does not pay enough attention to the arts. We cannot expect to maintain world leadership with cultural illiteracy. Students must have time to practice. There is nothing that requires as much attention in our schools today as music and the arts.

We must educate future citizens of the universe by the example we set here at Interlochen, by the American concept of free enterprise and motivation we promote here, and that means work, work, and work. . . . A taxi driver in New York once asked Van Cliburn, "How do you get to Carnegie Hall?," and Van said, "Practice, practice, practice." He started at age three. . . . We need new educational ideals instead of X number of hours spent in a classroom to avoid effort. Promotion by individual achievement seems to be in bad repute in this country. We need motivation and academic freedom to get to the top, but we can't let our morals go to pieces. . . .

PMA AT WORK

After W. Clement Stone became associated with Interlochen, he sometimes took the podium and tempered Joe Maddy's outbursts with a religious approach and a strong dose of PMA (Positive Mental Attitude) that tied everything together. They made a good team.

But long before he met Mr. Stone, Joe Maddy was extolling *The Amazing Results of Positive Thinking* by Norman Vincent Peale in his sermons. Dr. Maddy reached a zenith in the summer of 1954, when he ended his Sunday morning message with a startling announcement:

> Now I am going to let you in on a secret that not even my trustees know. You have laid the cornerstone for the future of American culture. On this eleven hundred acres there will be one of the greatest institutions for the development of the arts that the world has ever seen. A movement for mankind that is beyond comparison. Who can describe the Grand Canyon without seeing it? And even after you see it, how can you describe it? That is the concept of this great institution of learning that is going to be developed right here on this campus.

There was a silent shuddering in the audience, and a muffled voice said, "How in hell is he going to pay for it? He hasn't even paid for the last hole."

8
MACK . . .
A BEAN COUNTER'S WOES

"He spends tomorrow's money yesterday."

❧

Poor Mack. Everyone felt sorry for him. He was the book-keeper, camp treasurer, and chief bean counter whose job was to figure out how to pay for the holes, the hamburger, and the salaries.

Joe Maddy sniffed, "These kids never went hungry. There was always enough money for hamburger. And no-body missed their salaries but me."

George Mackmiller was a deacon in the First Presbyterian Church in Ann Arbor and a Phi Beta Kappa graduate of the University of Michigan's Business School. He was teaching commercial studies in the Ann Arbor high school and had built up his own successful accounting practice when Joe Maddy enticed him to come to Interlochen one summer and help straighten out the camp's bookkeeping. It was a mess.

"I don't know why I came. I didn't know from which

43

end to blow a violin. My salary that first summer was two hundred dollars for eight weeks. I brought my family and paid three hundred dollars for a cabin, and we bought our own food. I didn't do so well. But it was a great place for the kids," he recalled.

Years later he lamented, "I don't know why I stayed. My sons earn a lot more money than I do."

But he did stay. As someone said—and many felt, "Once you are here and get the feel for it, you are never the same again."

Mack admired Dr. Maddy for what he was trying to accomplish. But Mack didn't see him through the same rose-colored glasses that inspired others to perceive him as some sort of miracle man. Mack never minced words in interviews on the subject or in the memos he wrote to himself through the years. These were kept in a secret file. Only a few people knew about them. They contained some rhetoric reflecting Mack's gloomy outlook on the business of chasing million-dollar dreams.

Here are excerpts, quoted verbatim, from our discussions during the 1940s and 1950s.

IN MACK'S OWN WORDS

There is no one I have ever known who in such a short time could dream up more work for more people to do and turn it over to them, and then promptly turn around and start thinking of something else for them to do. Whatever anyone is involved in doing, Joe Maddy has no hesitation to barge in and ask you to drop what you are doing and start on something else. He always wants tomorrow's work done yesterday. He's full of piano wire, taut and tense and resilient.

But he has recently shown himself willing, when the evidence is almost overwhelming, to concede a point. Not often.

There are not enough bricks in the universe since before or after the pyramids were erected that if they would all fall at one time, they would ever have disturbed Joe Maddy's frame of mind.

He looks at this camp as his own, but it is a nonprofit educational institution created under certain laws of the state of Michigan without which it could not operate but which he doesn't recognize at all. He feels this sense of ownership, like he's omnipotent.

He always spends tomorrow's money yesterday, but he can always find good resources for it with his trustees. He doesn't let them forget the grievous mistakes they've made in turning him down on what he wanted to do. He's like an elephant. He never forgets.

He runs this camp on intuition, not facts and figures. If the figures don't come out the way he wants them, they're no good.

His confidence does not require him to pay any attention to me. If you put end to end the several times—small segments of time—that he spends with me over a year discussing the financial status of this organization, it would not total one eight-hour day.

I never advise him. This is not a wise thing to do. If he asked me, I'd tell him. As an officer in the corporation I have my responsibilities, and those are the things I'm supposed to take care of. But trying to tell Joe Maddy what is wrong—it goes off like water off a duck's back.

He is a very convincing individual and speaks persuasively in board meetings. When he has ideas that his trustees question, he machine-guns them through. If history repeats itself, his $150,000 ideas will cost twice that much.

He has a $300,000 loan to build Brahms and the new student center and still owes $140,000 on the women's dorm. He's trying to handle a $2 million a year operation on a nickel and always comes up with an overdraft. Whether we have money for hamburger tomorrow, that's a horse from another garage.

We need to put this place on solid financial footing. If he ran it the way it should be run, we would only have two cabins, but they would be all paid for.

I think it's admirable that he wants a year-round school for gifted kids, but it costs money.

These holes he digs are not inexpensive. He's chasing butterflies.

FROM MACK'S MEMOS

June 30, 1959 . . . The dazzling appearance of the National Music Camp's summer operations and the obvious enthusiasm demonstrated by the campers have misled and blinded both the trustees and management to a vital economic fact: That since the inception of the National Music Camp, had services of all kinds been compensated for at the market rate, the camp would not have grown to its present size if indeed it would have survived at all. If the financial success of the proposed winter school is predicated on the apparent financial success of the National Music Camp, that predication is founded on a false premise. In the building of the National Music Camp there has been expended a hell of a lot more blood, sweat, and tears than cement blocks, nails, and lumber.

Should a stranger to the quagmire of baffling and bewildering intricacies, which so well characterize the financial maze in which the National Music Camp operates, be asked to carry on because of the incapacity of the present assistant treasurer, there might be a long period before the railroad is operating smoothly again.

It is high time that the management of this enterprise become realistic. The expansion program is far underwritten, activities are being supported that cannot be afforded, money is being spent and committed that we do not have nor have any certainty of getting, and no attention has ever been paid to recommendations repeated regularly and often for more than four years that a minimum cash balance of no less than $100,000 is necessary just to carry on smoothly the normal day-to-day operations.

What to do? Get on a pay-as-you-go basis, and if you cannot pay, do not go.

November 3, 1959 . . . Extraordinary tranquillity and equanimity have been exercised and maintained while the edifice crumbled.

December 8, 1959 . . . I still think far too little money is in sight to do the things that are being planned and someone will not be paid on time, including workers.

47

Mack's Poem
I'm not allowed to run the train,
The whistle I can't blow . . .
I'm not the one who designates
How far the train will go.
I'm not allowed to blow the steam
Or even ring the bell,
But let the damn train jump the track,
And see who catches hell.

In a couple of years Mack's woes and worries would be somewhat alleviated by a sudden windfall.

9
CLEM, THE MAN BEHIND THE MUSTACHE WITH A HALO AROUND HIS HEART

He always greets people with a hearty "How's your PMA?"
and renews his own PMA daily by declaring at every
opportunity, "I feel healthy! I feel happy! I feel terrific!"

❧

So many people have asked how in the world Dr. Maddy, who wasn't the world's greatest salesperson, could sell a man like W. Clement Stone on giving millions to Interlochen.

This is how it happened. It was in August 1961.

Dr. Maddy had just come from a board of trustees' meeting, a little downcast. He put his arm around Don Gonzales, a longtime supporter of the camp, and said, "Don, the trustees have turned me down on the Academy. I'm going to have to go it alone."

A few hours later he stopped me on the steps of the administration building as I was heading back for Chicago and said, rather desperately, "I need some help. The trustees turned me down again. This time it's final. They won't let me open the winter school. We can't borrow any more money." He paused, then burst out, "Do you know anyone with money who could help get the school started?"

I had known him through one crisis after another, but

49

this time was different. There was a look of despair, almost panic, on his face that haunted me.

Of course in my newspaper work I'd met many people of wealth, influence, power. I interviewed them, wrote stories about them. But ask them for money? I wouldn't dare.

There was one man, however, who was different. He seemed to be always giving his money away to worthy causes. His name was W. Clement Stone. He was always good copy for reporters and a favorite of press photographers. With his well-manicured mustache, his colorful big bow ties, and omnipresent pre-Castro Cuban cigars that were and still are his trademarks, he looked like something between a croupier and a Mississippi riverboat captain. And he was—and still is—a dashing figure on the dance floor.

He was one of Chicago's most prominent business and civic leaders. His business was insurance (Combined Insurance Company of America), his philosophy was PMA (Positive Mental Attitude), and his hobby was philanthropy, giving money away.

In all the years I had known him, he had impressed me as a rather enigmatic but extremely kind man. His wealth was beyond my comprehension. All I knew was what I read in the newspapers. His public relations man, Lou Fink, was a close friend of ours, so one day I asked him, "Does Mr. Stone really have all that money to give away? Do you think he might give some to Interlochen?"

Lou said, "Why don't you ask him?" I said, "How?" He said, "Just ask him. I'll set up an appointment."

He did. And with fear and trembling I sat there on the

other side of a big desk, facing W. Clement Stone as if for the first time and pouring my heart out about Dr. Maddy's dream for a year-round school. He listened attentively, flicked his cigar, and said softly, "I'll be happy to see him. Ask him to send me a prospectus first."

I didn't even know what a prospectus was. When we left his office, Lou said, "You goofed. You should have asked for a specific amount. Mr. Stone likes specifics."

I wasn't in the fund-raising business. "How much should I have asked for?"

"About $8,000," Lou said. Oh well.

I phoned Dr. Maddy and told him to do a "prospectus"—whatever that was—with lots of *specifics*. I would never have guessed he could do his homework so well. It arrived, fourteen pages long, a financial report with detailed itemization of all the camp's debts and cost estimates of Joe Maddy's proposed Interlochen Arts Academy. These were in the $100,000 to $400,000 range, none for $8,000.

I sent it over to Mr. Stone, and he invited us to dinner at the Stones' villa on Chicago's north shore of Lake Michigan, in Winnetka. Dr. Maddy had practically memorized Mr. Stone's book *Success Through a Positive Mental Attitude* in order to be prepared to meet him.

He was imbued with PMA when we arrived. But his jaw dropped when we were ushered into a room filled with people. We had expected a private meeting with Mr. and Mrs. Stone. They greeted us warmly and introduced us to the other dinner guests. As we joined in the usual social-hour formalities, it seemed obvious that Mr. Stone had left no time to discuss Dr. Maddy's prospectus.

We were wrong. His timing was perfect. He glanced at

his watch, then quietly asked everyone to please be seated—in sofas and chairs surrounding a glass-topped coffee table. He drew up a chair for himself and one for Mrs. Stone beside him, facing the pre-dinner assemblage. In a courtly manner, he brought out the big sheaf of papers, held it up so everyone could get a good look at it, and said, "I would appreciate it if you will all listen carefully to Dr. Maddy's proposal." Then he passed it to Mrs. Stone and asked her to read it. Aloud!

Lou and I, with eye contact, stifled a groan. I felt an impulse to cry out, "No! Not here." I was so embarrassed for Dr. Maddy as he sat there listening to his financial problems being revealed to an audience of complete strangers. They must have been astounded at the amount of money this man Joe Maddy could spend on a little summer music camp in northern Michigan, when he didn't have it.

Even I winced. Mackmiller's bean counting hadn't prepared me for the shock of hearing it like this, through page after page of facts and figures on the camp's debts, how much had been spent on digging holes for new buildings, a new sewage system . . . and how much money they still owed the banks.

No one said a word. No one made a sound. Mrs. Stone went on with the second half of the prospectus, titled "Funds Needed for the Opening of the Interlochen Arts Academy."

Item Number One, demanded by the board of trustees, was *$300,000* to guarantee faculty salaries for the first year. Mr. Stone turned to Jessie and quietly interrupted, "You can skip that one, dear. We're taking care of that. Just go on to the next item."

Dr. Maddy, Lou Fink, and I did a quick double take with our eyes. Did we hear right? Still no one said a word. Mrs. Stone went on reading, with Mr. Stone interrupting occasionally to ask Dr. Maddy a question. There was another item, even bigger—$350,000 to complete the new sewage system.

Mrs. Stone finished reading the prospectus. Dinner was served and we adjourned again, briefly, to the living room for the thank-you and good-bye amenities. As we were getting ready to leave, Mr. Stone said to Dr. Maddy, "I'll send up written confirmation tomorrow for your trustees."

Dr. Maddy grasped his hand, practically jumping up and down, and blurted out, "Would you be one of our trustees?"

"I'd be happy to," Mr. Stone said.

Two months later he flew to Interlochen with Mrs. Stone for his first trustees' meeting. The camp was not in session. The grounds were deserted and bleak. Not much there except a bunch of holes. He couldn't possibly know what Interlochen was like.

But he wrote another check, this time for $350,000, to pay for the new sewage system.

The trustees were astonished. Who was this man Clement Stone? One of them asked him, "How can you do this when you know nothing about our institution?"

His reply: "I'm gambling on the man."

It wasn't until after many years, when we began our collaboration on this book, that I mustered the courage to tell Mr. Stone how Lou Fink had chastised me for not being specific and asking for $8,000.

Mr. Stone chuckled and said, "Now aren't you glad you didn't? Lou miscalculated, didn't he?"

Mr. Stone has given many millions to Interlochen over the years. He has contributed to other things he believes in as well—to religious, medical, and educational programs; to prison reform; to children's charities for the handicapped and retarded as well as the gifted; to the Boy Scouts of America (he is a former national president); to the National Committee for the Prevention of Child Abuse, founded in Chicago by his daughter Donna; to Dr. Karl Menninger's psychiatric clinic in Topeka, Kansas, and Dr. W. Grey Walter's scientific research in cybernetics at the Neurological Institute in Bristol, England . . . the list is endless.

But he had a soft spot in his heart for Joe Maddy from the first time he met him and knew that here was a man he would like to have as a friend and share in his dream.

The friendship blossomed. Interlochen became like a second home to Clement and Jessie Stone when they could find time to get away. Dr. Maddy even sweet-talked them into going deep-sea fishing with him off the Florida Keys. After camp was over, and when they could afford it, Dr. and Mrs. Maddy would haul their little trailer down to Marathon, Florida, for a week of indulging Joe Maddy's passion for deep-sea fishing. Mrs. Maddy didn't care much for it, but she was a good sport.

Her enthusiasm was regenerated when they took the Stones out on the boat one day and Mrs. Stone hooked a *very* big fish. They helped her reel it in. It was sixteen feet long, bigger than anything Dr. Maddy had ever caught. Mr. Stone was so thrilled that Jessie had caught it on her very first deep-sea fishing expedition. . . . He sent a thank-you letter with a check enclosed for $1 million.

There are many who still remember that million-dollar fish. Mr. Stone remembers it, too. What kind of fish was it? A long fish. A shark? No, but pretty big. Sixteen feet long. A million dollars? I think so. That's $60,000 a foot. Let the bean counters worry.

On a business trip to New Zealand, Mr. Stone befriended a struggling young Maori woodcarver, bought out his whole lot of primitive wood sculptures, shipped them to Interlochen, and gave the woodcarver a new lease on life and his art works. In Australia he discovered a talented young violinist who had heard about Interlochen and wanted to go there to study. But she was reluctant to leave her family. So he brought the whole family.

Mr. Stone served as board chairman from the early 1970s until 1989, when he stepped aside, at the age of eighty-seven, and assumed the title of honorary chairman. His passion for Interlochen was legendary, manifested by his years of service and unflinching willingness to donate funds. Some of the funds went for building a badly needed replacement for the old Interlochen Bowl Hotel. Dr. Maddy named it the Stone Student Center. "I didn't think it would be appropriate to name the new sewage system for him," he said.

Later, the Jessie V. Stone building was constructed adjacent to the Maddy Administration Building and connected by a long, wide, and beautiful corridor and exhibit hall called Giddings Concourse. The Jessie V. Stone building features an enormous and splendid auditorium and student performing center.

When Joe Maddy died, on April 18, 1966, his funeral

service was held in the Jessie V. Stone Auditorium, against a magnificent huge backdrop of pine trees, shrubs, and evergreens. The whole area was banked with Dr. Maddy's beloved pines. It was as though the forests outside were literally brought into the building.

Board member Don Currie, whose son and daughter-in-law were students there at the time, recalls, "It was one of my most poignant memories of Interlochen. The emotions of the students, parents, and staff, the sadness and yet the beauty of the music and the service—it was incredible. I will never go into the Jessie V. Stone building without thinking about it."

Dr. Maddy did live to see the fulfillment of his dream for a winter school. The Interlochen Arts Academy opened in September 1962, just a year after Clement and Jessie Stone first saw those big holes waiting for money to put buildings in them. They continued their support after his death. But there were some turbulent times ahead.

Don Currie remembers one of them vividly:

"We were in extremely bad financial straits, a real crisis. It was at the point where we were going to have to sell millions of dollars' worth of stock that Mr. Stone had given us. And we were in a position where we would have to sell it at a rate about one-third lower than its market value. A board meeting was called to take a vote on it.

"Mr. Stone never interrupted a voting issue, never tried to impose his weight as board chair to influence anyone's thinking. He sat quietly and listened to each side of the argument about whether to sell the stock or not. The vote was taken. The pro-selling side won. After it was over, Mr. Stone said very quietly, 'Now I would like for you to do me a favor. I would like for you to give me the opportunity of buying the stock back at its original value.'

"Now that is the measure of a really unselfish giver."

In the summer of 1975 Mr. Stone asked his friend Bob Hope to do a benefit performance at Interlochen. Bob Hope did not need much persuasion from W. Clement Stone. At the end of the concert he paid tribute to Mr. Stone with these words: "Some people think a halo is worn around the head. Here is a man who wears a halo around his heart."

Maybe Bob Hope has one, too. He donated his $25,000 performer's fee to Interlochen.

Mr. Stone celebrated his seventy-fifth birthday on May 4, 1977. Following is a letter from Fay Maddy dated April 3, 1977:

Dear Jessie and Clement Stone,

I feel highly honored to be invited to join in a tribute to you on the occasion of Mr. Stone's seventy-fifth birthday. My warmest congratulations and best wishes on this important day. But, how can I express what I feel in my heart for you—not only on this day, but every day. Your friendship, your generosity, your inspirational ideals, and your goodness, have touched many lives the world over. I know that none more than my husband, Joe Maddy, who, like you, had his own magnificent obsession named Interlochen and who, like you, believed in helping others and sharing himself with others through the universal language of arts. You came into our lives at a time of real crisis. You had faith in a man with an "impossible dream." You helped turn his dream into a reality, and today thousands of talented young boys and girls all over the world are contributing their own share of beauty and goodness, inspirational ideals, and leadership from their training at Interlochen. It was always Joe Maddy's philosophy that our young people should be trained for leadership in life as well as in the arts, that they could contribute to world peace and understanding, to the betterment of mankind, through the artistic, educational, and moral standards set at Interlochen. He died happy in the knowledge that his life's work would be carried on and his magnificent obsession shared with others.

Thanks to you, our dear friends, W. Clement and Jessie V. Stone. You are living proofs of your own philosophy. That which you share with others will multiply. It must give you a great sense of inner peace and pride on this special day to look back over the years and recall how some of the gifts you left along the way seem to multiply and spread and reap unknown harvests. I hope Interlochen will continue always to make you proud. You have done many good things for many worthwhile organizations and individuals, but for this special occasion, I would like to say a very special thank you for that. God bless you both.

With love and gratitude, Fay Maddy.

For his eightieth birthday, in 1982, she wrote:

I'll never forget the first time I met Mrs. Stone. It was the first time I went with Joe to call on Mr. Stone at his home. Joe went in and I sat waiting in the car until they sent for me. I fell in love with Mr. and Mrs. Stone the minute I met them. I already knew they were won-

derful people because of what they had done for Interlochen without even yet knowing much about it. But
Mr. Stone had said he did it because he believed in Joe.
I was curious because he barely knew Joe. I asked him
what there was about Joe that he liked and made him
believe in him. I'll never forget his reply. Mr. Stone said
he looked at Joe's shoes and noticed that they were
beautifully shined and so he knew that Joe was a gen-
tleman. I have many precious memories of both Mr.
Stone and Jessie, but this is one of my most precious. I
love you both.

    Fay Maddy.

    W. CLEMENT STONE is chairman emeritus of the
Aon Corporation, a vast insurance empire with operations
throughout the United States and the rest of the world. In
recent years, much of his time, energy, and money has been
devoted to philanthropy, civic activities, and political
causes. In 1981 he was a nominee for the Nobel Peace Prize
in recognition of his humanitarian and philanthropic work
on behalf of mankind. He holds eighteen honorary docto-
rates and numerous humanitarian awards, including the
Herbert Hoover Humanitarian Award and the Horatio Alger
Award. He is a member of the Republican National Finance
Committee and a member of the Republican Senatorial
Trust.

"One of my favorite Joe Maddy stories was written by a columnist in Grand Rapids, Michigan, and dated July 20, 1944. It starts out, 'Dr. Maddy says . . .,' and it's about a little boy who asked his father, 'Why can't I see in my ear with my eye?' The answer was, 'How do you know you can't? Have you tried? You'd better try. The harder you try, the sooner you will be able to. And, besides, Dr. Maddy says you can.'"

Gerald B. Fischer
Chief Executive Officer
University of Minnesota
Longtime member of the
Interlochen Board of Trustees
and three-time Interlochen camper

PART III
RETROSPECTIVE

THIS RETROSPECTIVE IS A PROFILE of Joe Maddy as captured in kaleidoscopic word pictures and vignettes, and told by those who knew him and worked with him. Most of the interviews here were conducted in 1975, some in 1991.

10
SONNY BOSSINGHAM

"I'm the guy who dug all the holes for him."

❧

They call me Sonny here, but my real name is Morris. Dr. Maddy gave me the name Sonny. He was almost like a father to me, though it took a while for us to get acquainted. I was here two weeks before I even knew who he was.

I was fresh out of the service and the youngest guy who worked here at the time. This was the spring of '46. I'd had a job running heavy equipment for the government before I went into the service and was told I could have my job back in ninety days if I wanted it. That's what I planned to do.

But I'd heard about this summer music camp and thought it would be a good place to pick up some extra money while I was waiting to go back to work—like a vacation.

A vacation? Well, they put me to work on the maintenance crew, and the only equipment they had then was an old worn-out bulldozer, one dump truck, an old cement

63

mixer, and an old Ford stake rack truck which they'd put benches in so people could ride into town to go to church on Sundays.

My first job was to fix the old broken-down bulldozer. I was in my early twenties and I had noticed this elderly fellow running around, talking to different workers, checking on things, asking questions. He was here, there, and all over. I thought, Gee, it's like he wants to know what's going on everyplace, what people were working on and what they were doing. I thought he must have something to do with this place.

One day he came around to me and asked what was the matter with the bulldozer.

"The main thing is it's worn out," I told him.

"Well, they tell me you're the guy who can make it run if anybody can," he said.

I liked his attitude. So I got to work on it, and I got it to running, and I started digging holes for dry wells and septic tanks and a lot of other things all over the place with that old bulldozer. I didn't know when I was talking to him that this was Joe Maddy. When you're in your twenties, you think of anyone over forty or fifty as "elderly," but he never did seem like an old man, the way he got around and was always doing things.

We finally got another piece of equipment, a little used Bantam crane to dig with. I hadn't run one of those things before, so a guy brought it up here and spent about two hours with me going over it, showing me how to use it. And then he left.

Dr. Maddy said, "Well, go ahead, Sonny, you can run it. Just take your time. You can run it. . . . Come on, we've got another job to do."

He never took "no" for an answer. So we ran the crane over to a piece of ground that hadn't been bulldozed, and I said, "Well, what do you want dug here?"

He said, "Well, just start digging a hole."

I asked, "What're the dimensions? What depth?"

He repeated, "Just start digging."

People would come by and see me digging, and they would ask, "What are you going to build there?"

Well, what could I say? I didn't know. They thought this was most peculiar.

Eventually Dr. Maddy told me, "We're going to build a new kitchen, a cafeteria for the Junior and Intermediate girls to eat in as soon as I get enough money. I'm just digging the hole now and by this fall we'll have enough money to start building. I'll tell you what size hole after I get the money."

As it turned out, the money, as usual, was a little slow in coming, but, also as usual, that didn't disturb Dr. Maddy one iota. He had planned the hole for a full basement under the building which is now Pinecrest, and to include the new kitchen. Instead, he put just a small basement under the kitchen, and then as time went by and money came in, we excavated the dirt from underneath the standing building, rebuilt, and added on, so now it has not only the kitchen but classrooms and things like that.

That was the way he did things. He would get an idea, always a good one, and I don't know of any job we started that we didn't finish. I've dug about 75 or 80 percent of the basements. I could never work for a better man.

He always appreciated it when you did a good job. He made you want to do it even better the next time, to improve on it. He made you feel that you wanted to give your best. He would talk to people about anything they were interested in, about the way their work was going, and if you had a better idea about how something should be done, he would listen to it, to anything. He wasn't like some bosses who come up and say, "I want you to do this or that, and I want you to do it right now." He always knew in his mind what he wanted, and he would come by and say, "This is what I'm trying to do and if you can help me, we'll get along better." He hated to see time wasted.

In the beginning I told him, "I'll work for you for two months. Then I'm going back to my old job."

He didn't want me to leave, especially after I'd run that bulldozer. He said, "You stick with me until this school gets to operating." Even back then he was planning to build the camp into a year-round campus. Everyone thought he was crazy. He said, "If you stay here and help me get this school going, I'll see that you get a permanent job, that you don't have to worry about anything."

I said, "Well, I'm only getting seventy-five cents an hour working for you, and I was making a lot more than that before I ever went into the service. And times have changed and prices are different."

He said, "I'll give you a little raise if you stay." Whether it was a nickel or a dime I don't know. Whatever it was, it was worth the pay I was getting just to watch him jumping up and down and clapping his hands when I lifted these big hunks of cement while we were digging the holes.

I would have been better off financially if I had gone back to my old job. But this man changed my life. I came here for two months and stayed forty years. I watched the camp grow—from some little violinist sitting here in the woods screeching away and some opera singer sitting on a stump screeching her head off. But Dr. Maddy loved these kids.

Sometimes I would go deer hunting with him, and then we would build a little fire and roast hot dogs and sit down and just talk. All he talked about was these kids and their music and what he wanted to do for them.

I'm satisfied that I stayed here. It wasn't for the money. It was the good feeling I had from being able to help him help these talented students. That was his main goal.

There were folks around in those days who liked to refer to Joe Maddy and his "tribe" as a bunch of jackpine savages. I am proud to have been one of them. The way I felt about him was like a buddy overseas—you'd lay your life on the line for him. Especially when you knew that the turkey in your Christmas basket was paid for out of his own pocket.

SONNY BOSSINGHAM was general foreman of the maintenance crew at Interlochen. He is now retired and lives in Traverse City.

11
PEG STACE

"He expected everybody to give their all, and most everybody did."

❦

When I first arrived here I thought it was the craziest place I'd ever seen. It was a hot Sunday, the dust was eight inches thick, and all these funny-looking people were running around in knickers. I knew this was the uniform. You realize that very quickly. I had to wear those knickers that first summer I was here, and I was lovely. They didn't meet anywhere in the rear. My own father didn't even recognize me when he came to visit. He tapped me on the shoulder and asked me where he could find Miss Stace.

I didn't know what my job was going to be. I brought my golf clubs. I thought I was going to have lots of time to do other things. Not a vacation exactly, but I didn't think it was going to be what it was. I was in the middle of everything that I knew nothing about. Dr. Maddy wanted to be relieved of some things. He needed an assistant, and he said it had to be someone who could answer questions. I made some mistakes, but he stuck by me. We always got out of situations gracefully. He told me I wouldn't do him any good if people didn't have confidence in me.

I remember that first summer, there was a doctor's wife who had two kids in camp and a million questions. Her kids came back for many years, and each year she would have more questions.

She used to write reams of letters with questions. She drove me mad. One day as we were going through the cafeteria line—this was about four years later—she said, "Now I told my husband that you were one person at Interlochen who really knows the answers. How long have you been here?" I told her I had been there twenty minutes before she came, and she never asked me another question.

The first summer was rough. Dr. Maddy was very cooperative and most helpful. But there were times when I wondered why I was there. I was very impressed by the people. I had expected a lot of long-haired geniuses. To my surprise they were very compatible and human.

Dr. Maddy had his own approach to things. The hole I remember best, mostly because it was such a shock to the board and all, was when he started excavating for the women's dorm. He got the hole dug before anybody could stop him. We were sure we had a high-class swimming pool on our hands. We were all utterly horrified. This was going to be a $250,000 to $300,000 building, and he didn't have the money to fill it. He always got himself into things and somehow got saved.

He never felt that there should be any money left over. You should always be working on next year's income. This could get rough sometimes. There were times when the officers wouldn't get their pay for a week or two during the winter.

We would tell him that we didn't think he should be

doing this or that. We were very conscious of the fact that something could happen and the camp could go under. Confronting him never helped, but your conscience felt better by saying something. Sometimes he would get real mad when we told him these things. There were mornings when I would walk into the office and wonder if I still had a job.

He never said "no" gracefully, so I would say it for him. I was the official "no" person for years. I'd walk across campus and wonder if anybody was going to talk to me. I got to a point where I would go over to the office before breakfast and talk to him. I would calm him down if he were ready to explode at people. He was never a patient person, especially when he thought people weren't doing their jobs.

He hated it when conductors would sit down during rehearsals. He thought they weren't giving it their all. He expected everybody to give their all, and most people did.

Everyone shared in camp duties. People were surprised when they walked into the cafeteria and saw Dr. and Mrs. Maddy and T. P. Giddings serving. Everybody did their part, and those who didn't weren't very popular.

In the early years it was a chore to balance the orchestra. We always had enough violin and piano players. Those were the most popular instruments. It came to a point where all the violinists were required to play the viola for a week, and they rotated each week. This kept the orchestra balanced. We also gave a lot of scholarships to students who played the string bass and bassoon, because these usually were youngsters too poor to buy their own instruments and they had learned to play on what their school had to offer. We offered them a work scholarship. In return

70

for their tuition, they were required to work one or two hours a day, depending on their musical load.

Dr. Maddy had his fingers in everything. He knew absolutely everything about the camp. We liked it when a new building was going up, because we always knew where to find him if we needed him. He would watch that building go up for hours. He'd also visit the classes. Beginner and Junior orchestra were his favorites. If you had to find him at a certain time of the day you could just follow the path he took according to the class schedule.

There was one memorable time when we couldn't find him when we needed him, though, and that was when the new Kresge Auditorium went up. He loved that building. Everyone did, but there was a great allegiance to the Interlochen Bowl.

Every time there was a cloud in the sky Dr. Maddy would move the concert to Kresge, whether it rained or not. The first dance concert came along, and Hildegarde Lewis, the dance director, loved the Bowl. She had planned all her choreography around the risers in the Bowl. The whole day had been wet. Not raining, but misting. We needed Dr. Maddy to make a decision on whether to move the concert.

He couldn't be found, so at 5:30 that evening we decided to move the concert to Kresge. It was a mess. The pit had never been taken out, and Hildegarde was having a stroke about her choreography. I finally found him on the catwalk above Kresge and asked him where he'd been. He grinned like a Cheshire cat, laughed that little-boy laugh, and said he'd been off campus—fishing. He didn't want to be the one to make the decision about whether it was going to rain and where the concert would be. Everyone got so mad at him when he would move the concerts and it

71

wouldn't rain. He didn't want that to happen again. You could forgive him for anything when he gave you that little-boy laugh.

PEG STACE is retired and lives on a golf course near Interlochen.

12
MELBA BRAM

"Work ethic? He didn't just preach it, he invented it."

꒝

I'll never forget the day I arrived. It was a beautiful morning. Everybody was so enthusiastic, as they always are when they are returning here. But I was new. I took one look at Faculty Row and thought it looked like a slum area. Well, grin and bear it. If I couldn't stand it I could always take my trumpet and go back to Wichita. I lived in H-1, the choice address on Faculty Row because it had a front porch. It also had two bathrooms for twelve staff and faculty people, one upstairs, one down. Sig Swanson, the trombone teacher, was always the hardest hit when the upstairs plumbing went out of whack. It was like Niagara Falls in his room. Charming.

One of my most vivid memories is of Russell and Maynard in their pajamas, foggy-eyed and rushing upstairs with brooms and things to take care of the bats.

I'd never been to camp. I don't quite know what I expected. I didn't expect that.

Obviously the place grew on me. After all these years I'm still here. Dr. Maddy's reaction to the bats was typical.

JOE MADDY OF INTERLOCHEN

He didn't acknowledge their existence. When we reminded him, as we often did, that some bats had taken up residence in our living quarters, he would twitch his mustache and say, with a twinkle in his eyes, "Don't worry. They won't hurt you. They're just little mice with wings." There were no boundaries or barriers to his overactive imagination. He was the original, certified, cockeyed optimist.

I first met Dr. Maddy while I was studying trumpet at the University of Wichita and playing in the college orchestra. He came there as a guest conductor. Everybody was impressed with his vitality and enthusiasm, in spite of the fact that he wasn't the world's greatest conductor. When he offered me a job at Interlochen, I accepted. Who wouldn't?

I was impressed with what he had done here to make it a success, in spite of all the obstacles, including the fact that he could be one of the most maddening people in the world to work with. He had the ability, like no one else I've ever known, to think in ten different directions at the same time. He just assumed that everyone was going to work twenty-four hours a day, the same as he did. We almost did.

I started with a four-hour-a-day job. It ended up twelve and eighteen hours a day. I audited classes. I played trumpet. I taught trumpet. I worked in the program office. I've done everything around here. I started as Peg's assistant. Everybody was Peg's assistant. She and a couple of other people ran the place, took care of the details while Dr. Maddy was out digging holes.

He had ideas. I don't know how much he slept because he would get these ideas in the middle of the night and scribble notes in the dark, then bring them to us to decipher the next morning, usually at 6:30 A.M. Someone gave him one of those flashlight pens so he could see what

74

he was writing when he had these flashes of ideas in the dark. It didn't help much. His writing was distinctive but not always legible.

He didn't just preach the work ethic, he invented it. He expected everyone to be up and bubbling at the crack of dawn. He did not like lazy people. One of the things he complained about the most was seeing conductors sitting on a stool at their rehearsals. He couldn't stand people sitting down on a stool. "This is a work camp, not a play camp," he always said. Loud and often. One very fine conductor was fired for being caught once too often conducting his rehearsals while sitting on a stool.

Dr. Maddy's ideas turned into some mighty big projects—and some of the biggest flops that anybody could ever conjure up. One of the first projects I did for him was a letter campaign trying to raise money, naturally. He gave me a *Who's Who* with a long list of names checked and a two-page letter asking for money. The letters had to be typed individually. This was in the days before the computer. The response was nil. No checks came in. The project fell flat. But by then he was into six others. He never acknowledged defeat. He didn't dwell on his flops. The only indication that he ever gave them a second thought was the fact that he rarely if ever made the same mistake twice. If the *Who's Who* idea didn't pan out—okay, he'd try another way.

A lot of people jumped to do whatever he wanted. He was so open and friendly and regarded all the staff, from kitchen to maintenance crew, not as employees but friends.

But we always shuddered before each of his radio talks or Sunday morning services. We didn't know what in the name of common sense he was going to say. But we knew he would drop a bombshell of some kind.

Dr. Maddy loved to fly. The car was too slow for him. Britt Gordon, one of our trustees, had a nice little plane. One day he invited me to come along with Dr. Maddy on a short flying sightseeing trip to the Upper Peninsula to see the new Mackinac bridge. On the way back, just after we crossed the straits, Britt said to Dr. Maddy, "Would you like to pilot the plane?"

It was hilarious watching Dr. Maddy doing body contortions to get into that pilot's seat, with his hand on the controls. It was a little bumpy. I guess the air up there is always turbulent anyway. But he did fine until we were nearly ready to land at the Traverse City airport, and he said, "I'd like to go out and see Interlochen from up here."

Britt said, "Fine."

So Dr. Maddy circled around Boys' Camp on Duck Lake and then headed for Kresge. He went up and down, buzzing the camp like it had never been buzzed before. He was always furious when other planes buzzed the camp. We skimmed the treetops and almost crash-landed on Kresge. I mean he really buzzed it. He was having a marvelous time. I've never seen such a look of rapture and enjoyment on anyone's face. But it was the most frightening experience of my life.

We finally flew back and landed at the Traverse City airport, then drove back to Interlochen with Dr. Maddy in his car. I've ridden with him in a car. But no more often than I had to.

Melba Bram was corporate secretary and administrative assistant to the president. She is now retired and lives on a golf course near Interlochen.

13
MARY FRANCES JAMES

*"This man could make you want to work your heart out
for him. He was a salesman of dreams."*

🌿

I've been with Interlochen since 1949. I drove here on a
cold day in June. I thought I had come to the end of the
world. It was awful. When I arrived, I was assigned to live
in the old H-1. What I remember most about H-1 was the
bats!

But after the first day the place got better. The friend-
liness of the people and the close living brought warmth
and a sense of family. We were truly a community in those
days. We shared the good and suffered the bad—living
conditions, bats, and all.

I was in awe of Dr. Maddy at first, just sort of in awe,
even afraid to speak to him. I was a greenhorn and he was
the big man.

I quickly learned that this was one of the greatest
things that had ever happened to me. I could hardly wait to
come back the next year. I played and taught flute and
bassoon. I liked working with kids, and these were a special breed of kids. They would soak up anything you could

pour into them, like a sponge. They were something special.

There is something I have never understood, and I still don't. They call it the "magic of Interlochen." It's an intangible thing that you just can't spell out. Something electric in the air that let me know that first summer—this is the place I've got to be.

Dr. Maddy was a salesman of dreams. Tangible things are hard enough to sell for some people, but ideas are harder. They are almost impossible, except to Dr. Maddy. He would never accept defeat. He turned defeat into a learning experience and went on from there. He never looked back and always went forward.

I remember one winter day when Dr. Maddy and I were looking at some office equipment in Traverse City, and he got a phone call telling him that building C-12, a minor performing area, had collapsed. The snow had built up and the roof had just caved in. He laughed and rubbed his nonexistent mustache and said. "Well, it wasn't big enough anyway." By the next summer he had a stronger, bigger building in its place.

He wouldn't take "no" for an answer. The trustees told him he couldn't build the girls' dormitory. That didn't stop him. He knew that somewhere he would find the money. He had the hole dug for it anyway.

He always knew what was going on. He didn't just let people go on a project. He knew exactly how things were progressing. He didn't check on you in a manner you were conscious of, but he jolly well knew what was going on. He always surrounded himself with people who knew what they were doing and he would trust their judgment.

He never bothered himself with specifics, though. He

had more dreams to come up with. He didn't have time to mess around with a lot of details, but he could tell you a lot more than most people.

I hope people who didn't know Dr. Maddy don't think those of us who did are living in the past when we talk about his qualities. It is not a matter of living in the past. It is a matter of trying to make an impression on other people as he did on me. Turning any bad situation into something good was one thing that impressed me. I wouldn't do it exactly the same way, but I certainly would make every effort to try. We are not living in the past. He wouldn't have wanted us to.

Dr. Maddy didn't make a conscious effort to brainwash you, but you couldn't escape the spell of him, of this place. This man could make you want to work your heart out for him. He was the kind of man you would knock yourself out for.

MARY FRANCES JAMES was administrative assistant to Dr. Wilson. She is now retired and lives near Traverse City.

14
TEX PAYNE

"There was never any doubt that you could do anything."

🌿

My name is really Frank J. Payne. I got the nickname Tex right here at Interlochen from Dr. Maddy, because I was from El Paso, Texas.

I played first oboe in the student orchestra in El Paso. I was good enough to win a scholarship from the El Paso high school to come up here. It was 1930, the third year of camp. It was a great honor to come here and be able to play music all summer long. I was seventeen. I thought I wanted to be a musician. Well, at least I wanted to find out whether I *could* be a musician, and it's one thing I *did* find out— fast!

At the end of my first week here, I wound up twelfth chair oboe out of twelve oboe players. That's a lot different from being first oboe in El Paso. Having come on a scholarship, I was wondering how I could show my face back in Texas, and I decided to do two things: improve my oboe and look around for something else. I had done some singing. I came from a singing family. I was pretty good at it. Maybe I could do some singing at Interlochen.

I'll never forget my first Monday night orchestra sight-reading session in the Bowl. We all went up on the stage and here on our stands was Dvořák's *New World Symphony*. I had never heard of it. I don't think many of the others had either. Where I came from, we worked several weeks on a relatively simple number. We hadn't heard much of this type of music in El Paso.

Dr. Maddy got up on the podium, rapped his baton and said, "Now we're going to play the *New World Symphony*."

And we did.

That was my first impression of Dr. Maddy. With him there was never any doubt that you could do anything. This place has never wasted any time on whether it was possible to do things. You just do them. It may take longer for some people than for others, but you *can* do it here.

I did improve my oboe, but I never got beyond seventh chair. The next two years I came back as a swimming instructor and Boys' Camp counselor.

One late Sunday afternoon, about the middle of camp session, I got a call from Dr. Maddy. He said, "Tex, get your bathing suit on and put your uniform on, and get over here to the hotel and come down to the dock." He always talked fast, like a popping firecracker. I asked, "What's up?" He said, "I've got two whole busloads of high-school kids here looking over the camp, and I want them to stay for the concert and we've got to entertain them and keep them around. You and I are going to put on an aquaplane demonstration."

I'd never heard of an aquaplane. Maybe I'd seen them in newsreels, but I didn't have the vaguest idea how to ride or operate one. Someone had given Dr. Maddy a nice little Criscraft inboard motorboat to run around in and take the kids for outings on the lake. We called it *Largo Fortissimo* because it was slow and very loud.

Dr. Maddy rigged it up as an aquaplane—which I now know was a forerunner of water skis—with a board tied onto the back of the boat and a rope hooked to the front end. He got in the boat and I got on the board, and he said, "When you want to go right, press more with your right foot, and when you want to go left, press with the left. . . . Now we're going to come around and I want you to swing out, really give them a show, go back and forth over the waves."

I never thought I could even get on one of those things. I was a good swimmer, not afraid of the water, but to do this and do it for an audience . . . well. But I did it, and it was pretty good. The kids stayed for the concert.

It was Joe Maddy's fantastic can-do attitude that inspired everyone to do their utmost for him.

I didn't do so well musically at Interlochen, but maybe I helped raise a little money with the Blanket, as it was called in those days. After Sunday evening concerts, there would be a blanket draped over the ticket booth, and people leaving would toss in coins and maybe dollar bills as their contribution to the camp. There was always a little extra entertainment around the Blanket to attract people's attention.

I was one of the Blanket entertainers, playing guitar and singing cowboy songs I grew up with in Texas. I wore a cowboy hat and my dad's cowboy boots, and after listening to that symphony stuff down in the Bowl, people would stop and listen to my cowboy music. And maybe drop a quarter in the blanket.

TEX PAYNE later won scholarships to New Mexico A & M and to Carleton College in Minnesota, where he graduated with a degree in physics, and became successful as a director of television commercials. His wife is an artist and successful dress designer. Their two daughters are former Interlochen students. He says he owes his success to Interlochen.

15
RICHMOND, INDIANA
Marcia Weissgerber Palmer, Julie McGuire, and Dave Marvel

≽

Joe Maddy's work as supervisor of music in Richmond, Indiana, was a crucial turning point in his career as one of the leading music educators in America. The historical details are recorded in my 1963 book *Joe Maddy of Interlochen.*

Following are taped interviews, from 1974, with three who knew him from those Indiana roots from which Interlochen sprouted.

MARCIA WEISSGERBER PALMER

"I just wish every youngster I have known could have been exposed to someone like Joe Maddy."

≽

I was a violinist, but I was hired at Interlochen as a lifeguard. Dr. Maddy said, "We need a lifeguard more than we need another violinist." That was the only job open, and I needed the money. My salary was $200, and room and board for eight weeks.

That was the summer of 1934, still Depression years. I didn't have a car, so I came by bus from Richmond, Indiana. Dr. Maddy had told me to get off at Chum's Corner and he'd meet me. I can still remember it as though it were only yesterday. I got off the bus with my violin under one arm and my suitcase in the other hand and my bedroll at my side.

I called the camp from Chum's Corner to be picked up. Everybody who came by bus had to be met at Chum's Corner, an intersection about three miles from Interlochen.

Dr. Maddy was in a meeting at Boys' Camp. There were no telephones at Boys' Camp at that time. The hotel switchboard operator told me just to wait at Chum's Corner and someone would run over and give him the message. He arrived, picked me up, and drove me out to camp. He was chattering all the way. "Now you're going to love working the waterfront," he assured me, "and you'll still have time to play the violin."

I told him I was a good swimmer but I had never expected to be working as a lifeguard. I'd had no experience at it. "You'll learn," he said confidently.

He took me to my cabin. I was assigned to the top bunk in Cabin 1, right across the road from the high-school girls' headquarters. As he left, he remembered to tell me, "Oh, yes, you're going to be a girls' counselor, too. You'll be in charge of morning set-ups. Get up and take the girls through their exercises at 6:30 A.M., right after bugle wakeup."

I'd never done anything like that in my whole life. I'd have to figure this out. I did. And I worked the waterfront as a lifeguard. It was quite an experience. I loved every minute of it.

And I just adored Joe Maddy. I practically worshiped him. I had known him since I was a child in Richmond, Indiana. I would have done anything he asked me to do—and there wasn't much he didn't ask me to do during all the summers I came to Interlochen.

But that first summer was crucial for me. I had a college degree in music education, but jobs were hard to find then.

I decided that Interlochen was going to be my salvation. It was either going to make me or break me. At the end of the summer, I did get a job as a music teacher in a little town in Ohio. It was a crummy school. But at least I had a job. And I had a better one each year from then on, teaching music in the public schools.

I came here every summer. I took the course in "How to Teach Singing" from T. P. Giddings. I took string quartet, I took harp, I took beginning woodwinds, and I took every college course that was offered.

Every summer I was here, I played in the orchestra. I continued studying violin, too. There was never a time when I wasn't in music here. But my jobs were of a great variety. There wasn't much I didn't do.

One summer I ran the hotel; another I worked the hotel switchboard. I ran the concession shop. I worked the ticket booth at concerts. I was one of the blanket holders for John Minnema, who was in charge of the Blanket fund-raising at concerts. We would take the tickets as people came in and hold the blanket as they came out, while they threw the quarters in.

There were four of us holding up the blanket. It wasn't

tied to anything. Usually when Mr. Minnema or Dr. Maddy asked for the money, they would say, "Now I don't want to hear any clanging of change. Make it a silent offering."— meaning to throw in paper money. There was always some entertainment to bring people to the Blanket, sometimes a little brass quartet, or Tex Payne playing the guitar and singing cowboy songs.

There wasn't ever a time when Dr. Maddy wasn't asking for money for something—to rent music, buy instruments, build a cabin. He never asked for anything for himself; it was always for the students. He never asked anybody to *do* anything for him, either. Whatever you did, you were doing it for yourself, to improve your own talent and abilities and opportunities. I think it is important for youngsters to realize that they need to work hard and learn, not just to please their teachers but to be better prepared for the future.

I just wish every youngster I have known could have been exposed to somebody like Joe Maddy.

As far as I am concerned, everything that Dr. Maddy had to offer was preparing me for the future. And it started a long time ago.

My love affair with Joe Maddy started when I was eleven years old and he first put a violin in my hands. He had come to Richmond to be supervisor of music and he was having tryouts to see what instruments the pupils could play.

I was in elementary school. I had started piano when I was eight years old. I had always wanted to play the violin because my Sunday school teacher played the violin. I was scared to death. I didn't think I was good enough. But I wasn't scared after I got started.

This new music man—he was Mr. Maddy then—was so warm and understanding. He understood children. He knew how to put the instrument in your hands and make you feel right holding it.

To this day I can remember his putting the violin in my hands. He adjusted my hand and my chin and the bow and made it feel right for me.

We had classes every week, once a week, after school. Then we began playing together in little recitals. The next year I was in junior high and we met during the noon hour. We had an orchestra then, with full instrumentation— oboe, bassoon, flute, string bass, everything that's important for a balanced orchestra. Before I left junior high, we had not only one, but an A and a B orchestra, and the same in senior high. When Joe Maddy had his first National High School Orchestra in Detroit, in 1926, the nucleus of that orchestra was from the Richmond High School A orchestra, about nineteen of us.

But I was the only one invited to play in his national orchestra in Dallas, in 1927.

In the beginning there was a big upheaval in Richmond over what Joe Maddy was doing. He had a terrible time with the school board because he didn't have a degree. He couldn't raise money for the things he needed.

The private teachers thought they were going to be put out of business because he was putting all of their piano students on other instruments and giving them *free* instruction in the public schools. The idea of group classes in schools was new to them. So was the idea of transferring a piano student to oboe or bassoon or violin. The piano students were the logical ones to go to orchestra instruments because they had the necessary background in training and reading music. There was no reason you had to give up one instrument in order to take up another unless that was your preference. The two go together. In fact, most people end up playing half a dozen instruments if they are really good. Joe Maddy knew that—but the town didn't.

He found many discarded instruments in attics and basements. Most of them he repaired himself. If he wanted something done, he did it.

At Interlochen, I organized and conducted the first Intermediate Orchestra because Dr. Maddy asked me to do it. I liked the challenge. I had always secretly wanted to be a conductor. He never changed anything I ever did, never came and told me to do anything differently.

He recommended me for a teaching job in Atlanta, Georgia. Among other things in his letter he said he thought I was the finest woman orchestra conductor in the United States. That was an exaggeration, of course. But the letter was very special for me.

There was no orchestra in the high school in Atlanta when I arrived there. No one playing the clarinet, the oboe, flute, or bass. There were a few violins and maybe one or two cellos. I had to teach everybody in the orchestra everything, and it was only because I'd learned it from Joe Maddy and the people who worked for him that I was able to do it. I did the same thing there, in Atlanta, that he did in Richmond, only many years later. I didn't have to go out and get the money for it because the money was provided by the school board. I didn't have to scrounge and campaign for support the way Joe Maddy did because I was hired to do this.

I was in Atlanta from 1940 to 1946, as conductor of the

Atlanta Youth Symphony, and at Interlochen during the summers.

Next to my father, Joe Maddy was the strongest and most important influence on my life. He was like a second father to me. Whenever I had a problem of any kind, I always felt I could go and discuss it with Dr. Maddy and he would give me an answer that might be helpful. As far as I was concerned, it was always the right answer. I even went to him with personal problems. One came up that was *very* personal.

I fell in love with the camp doctor. He was Dr. Fred Palmer, fresh out of medical school at the University of Michigan, and Dr. Maddy had enticed him to come to Interlochen for a summer before looking for a job or setting up his own medical practice, which was his goal.

He came here to supervise the summer program at the camp's medical center. He came for only one summer, but like so many people who come here for only one summer, he fell under the spell of Joe Maddy's dream. I met him that summer, his first summer here. He came back the next summer and proposed to me. Interlochen is a very romantic place.

We debated how to break the news to Dr. Maddy that we were going to be married. After all, most husband-wife faculty members were already married when they were hired, and budding romances between students were quickly nipped in the bud by T. P. Giddings. We weren't students, but we didn't want T.P. wiggling his finger at us.

Joe Maddy gave us his blessing in typical Joe Maddy fashion. "Wonderful," he said. "Congratulations. Now, you know I'm digging this hole for the new girls' dormitory and

I've got an idea. . . . Just be sure you're back here next summer."

How could we not be?

MARCIA WEISSGERBER PALMER is now retired and lives in Green Valley, Arizona.

JULIE McGUIRE

"He conned me into doing a harp cadenza with one chord."

I was born in Richmond, Indiana, to a very musical family. My father conducted the community orchestra and chorus, my mother played the church organ, my four brothers and sister all played different instruments, and I played the piano. We had our own little family orchestra at home.

I went away to college, then came back to Richmond in my first job—as Joe Maddy's assistant supervisor of music in the public schools. I had never met Joe Maddy but I liked him very much from the start. And why shouldn't I? He was a marvelous person to work with. He made me feel that I had carte blanche to do whatever I wanted. He didn't question anything. I made out my own curriculum. I taught harmony, music appreciation, orchestration, and conducting, and I had charge of the B orchestra. He had the A orchestra, which of course was the best.

Whenever he needed a bassoon or oboe or horn of some type, he would come to the B orchestra and pick out

91

my best students to go and play in his A orchestra. I was always losing them.

What impressed me most of all was his creativity in conning kids to play any instrument he needed for a concert. Joe Maddy was a con artist of the highest order. He had the fantastic ability of selling anybody on the idea of doing anything just by saying, "You can do it."

He even conned me into doing a harp cadenza with one chord when I couldn't play the harp, knew nothing about a harp, had rarely even seen one, and had absolutely no interest in harps. They were for the angels.

By the beginning of his second year in Richmond, Joe Maddy had built up a fine symphony orchestra with very good instrumentation. The only instrument missing in his orchestra was the harp. In fact, there wasn't a harp or a harpist for miles around. The closest one was in Indianapolis. Nobody in Richmond was willing to spend a thousand dollars or so for a harp and then go to Indianapolis to learn how to play it. But Dr. Maddy wanted a harp in his orchestra.

He explained to the students why they needed one to complete the instrumentation. He asked them to help him raise the money to buy a harp. They went out and sold season tickets for six concerts by their orchestra at a dollar each and raised four hundred dollars. Dr. Maddy sent word to instrument manufacturers that he had four hundred dollars with which to buy a harp, and could anyone furnish him with one at that price? Lyon and Healy in Chicago came through. They gave him a seven-hundred-fifty-dollar harp for four hundred dollars. There was still nobody to play it.

We had an upcoming concert in Portland, Indiana, and

Dr. Maddy wanted to show off that harp. So he invited Pasquale Montani, a fine harpist from Indianapolis, to be guest artist and deliberately planned the program to feature the harp, with orchestral accompaniment. The music included Debussy's Prelude to "The Afternoon of a Faun" and Rimsky-Korsakov's *Capriccio espagnol.*

Then he hit me with a surprise. "Julie," he said, "you're going to play the harp in the orchestra." I was stunned. The harp was brand-new. It had just arrived. We only had a week to rehearse for the concert. Besides, I wasn't even in his orchestra. I only played piano.

"But Dr. Maddy," I said, "I don't know the first thing about a harp. And I can't learn in a week."

"You play the piano. You can read music. And you should never use that word *can't*," he scolded. "I don't know how to play a harp either, but I know enough to show you how to work the pedals and pluck the C and G chords. That's all you need to know.

"Besides," he added, "think how it will look to the audience. The kids will love it. The parents will love it. I'm the conductor, you're my assistant supervisor and conductor of our B orchestra, and it's just logical that you should be the harpist up there showing off our new harp. It will make the harp look good, and you, too."

His brown eyes sparkled with excitement. How could anyone resist him?

He showed me how to push the pedals for the C and G chords and how to strum the strings. Mr. Montani, the guest artist, played a concerto with orchestral accompaniment, and he played the harp parts to the entire program. My contribution was more for effect than real music. I just sat there pushing the pedals and strumming away so people would think I was playing—except for one number in which I had to do a cadenza, and I really played it, but only in one chord. That was my solo to show off our beautiful new harp. I had learned it in only a week.

Dr. Maddy was right. Everyone was very impressed. At the end of the concert he announced that any student who wanted to take lessons could practice on our new harp for no charge except a share in the cost of strings. Furthermore, he said, Mr. Montani himself would come to Richmond once a week to give lessons.

Ten students signed up that night. In a few days there were sixteen. He called Lyon and Healy again and asked if they would *lend* him ten more harps for the school, on his personal guarantee against damage. To everyone's amazement, they did. Such were Joe Maddy's hypnotic powers of persuasion.

By the end of the school year he had an outstanding harp ensemble of eleven players. Most were piano players and learned quickly. The Richmond harp ensemble became widely recognized by music educators, and because of it Joe Maddy started another new movement—harp classes in schools.

I wasn't the only one who ever played "let's pretend" for this man. When he first came to Richmond, he had trouble finding enough instruments. But as enthusiasm and support for the orchestra increased, he gradually acquired more instruments than players in some categories. At one point he had twelve string basses but only eight players. So he nabbed four husky students, gave them a fast how-to-do-it, and had them stand back there and move their bows back and forth with the others, just to pretend they were playing. He always wanted the orchestra to look good in all the sections.

He always had his eye out for someone to play, especially the large instruments such as string bass and tuba. They were not as popular as the flute or violin, which were easier to carry. Any time he spotted a big boy walking down the hall, he would corner him and ask, "How would you like to play in the orchestra?" Then he would take him into his office and show him the basics of playing a certain instrument. Sometimes he kept the students so long that they were late for their next class. The other teachers weren't too happy about that.

There was one student, Perry Botkin, who was always roaming the hall and disrupting classes with his loud voice. He wasn't a very good student. One day Dr. Maddy collared him and said, "I'm going to take you to the principal's office." On the way, he noticed that Perry had big biceps. He asked, "How would you like to play the bass fiddle?"

Perry played banjo and ukelele. He wasn't interested in playing bass fiddle in the school orchestra. But he quickly decided it was better than going to the principal's office. He was in enough trouble already. So he became one of the orchestra's best string-bass players and years later a very well-known musician—and very rich—as string-bass player, guitar soloist, and orchestra manager for Bing Crosby. He probably wouldn't have been so successful if Dr. Maddy hadn't taken him on a detour from the principal's office.

One time Dr. Maddy needed a bassoon player for a certain concert, and with no trouble at all he spellbound a big boy into taking lessons on the bassoon, considered one of the most difficult of all instruments. Another time it was the oboe.

Many of his students went on to become professional musicians with big symphony orchestras. He really put Richmond on the map in the music world.

JULIE McGUIRE now lives in Naples, Florida.

DAVE MARVEL

"No other teacher made such an impression on me."

I was twelve years old when Joe Maddy came to Richmond. His presence there had an impact on thousands of people, and I happened to be one of them. Even at that early age, I thought he was a very fine conductor, a fabulous musician, and absolutely the most terrific clarinet player I'd ever seen or heard.

So I took up clarinet, thinking maybe I could be half as good as he was if I practiced hard. My father bought me a clarinet, but he didn't expect it to become an obsession. He was a surgeon and he wanted me, when I grew up, to go into medicine and be a doctor.

Everyone loved Joe Maddy. At that time it was customary for our high school to have a weekly chapel, during which time we always had a speaker, some entertainment, and announcements for the students. Our entertainment was often Joe Maddy on his clarinet or his gold-plated B-flat tenor sax that the Conn Instrument Company had given him, and he played clarinet and sax like nobody had ever heard anyone play. Before he came to Richmond, he had played in Isham Jones's jazz band in Chicago.

During our orchestra rehearsals he would pick up the first violin or second violin and demonstrate how he wanted a part played, without ever looking at the music. He seemed to have a masterful mind for notes and the memory of any music we were rehearsing. He never looked at the score. He already knew it.

I was in his A orchestra, but I also played in his band for the football games. I have vivid memories of coming into his office on Saturday mornings and seeing him sitting there writing out cards in longhand for each band member for a special piece he wanted us to play. I doubt if many people could sit down and write from memory as fast as he could the music we would be playing a couple of hours later.

I took clarinet lessons from him. At times it was diffi-cult to keep up with him. Without batting an eye and without any practice, he would show me exactly how he wanted something played, and it always amazed me how he could very simply play *anything*.

We rehearsed in the orchestra an hour each day, for which we received full credit, the same as an hour of English or history. He managed to get that through the state legislature or other proper sources. In addition, he would often get us to rehearse on Saturday mornings or Sunday afternoons.

We had to keep track daily of the number of hours we practiced, and it was nothing for me to play or practice four or five hours a day. He had us all so excited when he put these symphonic pieces in front of us. They were difficult,

97

things we had never played before. My ambition then was to play clarinet in a really *big*, important symphony. Like the Philadelphia Symphony. At that time it was the number-one symphony in America.

I had neglected my studies, given up athletics, and was spending all my time playing the clarinet—and oboe and saxophone, which Dr. Maddy had also taught me. After the clarinet, the sax was a breeze, but the oboe was difficult.

I had no time for anything but practice, practice, practice. I loved it. But my parents were horrified. They didn't want me to become a professional musician. At that time the only jobs for musicians were in the theater arts or symphonies. My parents thought music was for sissies, so they packed me off to a Quaker school where there was no music.

Whoosh! Bang! My dream was smashed.

I didn't finish high school in Richmond. I'm probably one of the few of Joe Maddy's early students in Richmond who didn't turn out to be a professional musician. Instead, I went into business and became head of one of America's biggest corporations. But the impact and memories of those early days in Richmond never left me.

I went to concerts at every opportunity and listened to the music of great composers whose works I had first heard in Richmond. From a distance, I followed Joe Maddy's career and I knew about Interlochen. My company began sending contributions. And one of the proudest moments of my life was when Dr. Maddy asked me to be on his board of trustees.

As a successful businessman, I could afford to become a "collector." I collected clarinets, many handmade in Paris

98

with special mouthpieces. They're still in great shape, and after fifty-five years I can still play them.

Until his death in 1988 DAVE MARVEL remained an active member on Interlochen's Board of Trustees and one of the school's strongest supporters. He was an officer in the Olin Company, a metal manufacturing firm based in St. Louis, which made significant contributions to Interlochen, largely because of Dave's early association with Joe Maddy in Richmond, Indiana. This interview was taped in 1975.

16
MINERVA TURNER

"Sometimes a guest would hold up the tray and say, 'Isn't this quaint?' "

❦

One day in the spring of 1947, my husband, Wendell, got a call from the director of food service at Michigan State University, in East Lansing, asking how we would like to go up to a little horn-tooting town in northern Michigan for the summer.

A man named Joe Maddy was looking for someone to run his cafeteria at Interlochen. Wendell was an expert in food service management. I was a dietitian and a frustrated, would-be musician. I played piano a little. I had heard about Interlochen. Many of my friends had been there. I was thrilled at the thought of spending a summer vacation there.

A vacation?

Wendell asked Dr. Maddy, "Do you mind if I hire my wife as dietitian?"

"Certainly not. We have lots of husbands and wives working here."

So suddenly I'm behind a food counter dishing out

food on aluminum trays to hundreds of kids in blue corduroy knickers and knee socks, with a staff of student helpers singing harmony loud and exuberantly as they slapped the food on the trays. Occasionally a startled guest would hold up the tray quizzically and say, "Isn't this quaint?"

The trays were Wendell's idea. Originally the camp was using old beat-up china that got broken by the boys in the dish room. At the end of our first three days we had three garbage cans filled with broken dishes. That's when Wendell asked Dr. Maddy, "Do you mind if we use mess trays?" They were the compartmented, stainless-steel trays used by the Navy during the war. We had used them at Michigan State.

Dr. Maddy thought about it and said, "How would the guests like eating off trays like that?"

Wendell asked, "Is this camp for the guests or the campers?"

"The campers, of course," Dr. Maddy said. So we got the trays.

We asked what we were supposed to do, what kind of food should we serve, what was our budget?

No budget, no problem, just give the kids the best food you can and keep them happy, he said.

He and Mrs. Maddy had some old-fashioned ideas. They would buy bushels of potatoes in the fall and put them in the basement. By summer when the students came, the potatoes had grown long sprouts on them and couldn't be used. Then he bulldozed someone into buying him a strawberry farm over on Gonder Road. But after one season when the strawberries didn't do very well, and the crop was on and off within a week, he decided it wasn't too practical.

101

When we first came, there were old oil-burning lamps in the kitchen and oil stoves that had to be heated an hour ahead of time in order to serve a meal. As soon as money could be scrounged and equipment could be found at low cost, the kitchen was converted to gas ranges and more modern appliances. We were finally able to afford big soup kettles and a few other things needed to serve a big group. Up to the time we came, the cafeteria had just been making do, mostly with things from Henry Ford's boats, including the food counters.

When we renovated the kitchen, I decided to revamp the cafeteria lines. I wanted a three-line cafeteria. Wendell said, "I don't think there is such a thing." Dr. Maddy said, "Well, just make one." So we did. There were a few bottle-necks in the beginning, but they soon smoothed out and the three cafeteria lines worked beautifully. One was for the high-school campers, another for the staff and faculty, the third for college students, visitors, and All-Staters. (The All-State students were those who came from Michigan for only a two-week program.)

The three lines were very close together, so we had lots of good music during meals.

When Dr. Maddy built Pinecrest, the Junior and Inter-mediate girls' dining room, he said, "I want two cafeteria lines here." Wendell said, "Well, Dr. Maddy, you don't need them. You're not going to have enough people to fill two lines." Dr. Maddy said, "You make them and I'll get the people." And he did.

He switched the All-State girls to Pinecrest for meals, which took a load off the hotel lines, and of course with better facilities the Junior and Intermediate Girls' Camp enrollment increased, and in a few years we were feeding

102

six hundred fifty to seven hundred girls over at Pinecrest. Dr. Maddy was right. We really needed two lines. It was this kind of vision that amazed everyone.

A cafeteria dining room is a great place to study the behavior and attitudes of people. Dr. Maddy had a very democratic philosophy. He could have had anything specially prepared for him if he wanted it. He never asked for special favors. The only thing we ever did especially for him in the food line was to have a bowl of potato chips under the counter when we had potato salad, because he couldn't eat anything with mayonnaise in it. So we always had potato chips for him.

I was a dietitian in a hospital in Detroit for a while, and the superintendent always had an entirely different—and better—meal than the staff and interns got. Neither Dr. Maddy nor Mrs. Maddy ever made any special demands, and almost every day they would take time to go into the kitchen and say hello to everybody and tell them what a great job they were doing. They treated everyone like friends, not employees.

Dr. Maddy had a hearty appetite. He enjoyed his food. He and Mrs. Maddy usually came through the line early, to beat the crowd, because people were always interrupting him at mealtime to talk or ask questions. Once I heard Mrs. Maddy say, "Joe, weren't you supposed to meet Mr. So-and-So here at twelve o'clock for lunch?" They were just finishing lunch, and Dr. Maddy had his mouth full of food. He mumbled, "If I waited for everybody who wanted to see me, I'd never get to eat."

He loved watermelon. One day he was in the line right ahead of Wendell. The girls were always instructed to give everyone the largest piece of melon that was on the serving tray at the time. For some reason Wendell got a larger piece than Dr. Maddy did. Dr. Maddy looked at Wendell's tray enviously, and like a hurt little boy said, "How come you got a bigger piece of watermelon than I did?"

Wendell said diplomatically, "I don't like watermelon very well anyway, so I'll change with you."

Dr. Maddy said, "Good!" and quickly reached over and changed pieces.

Most of our food service staff participated in camp activities, and sometimes their work hours conflicted with special events they needed or wanted to attend. At these times the regular staff and faculty would come in and substitute for them, working on the line at the serving tables. Dr. and Mrs. Maddy never hesitated to offer their help, and T. P. Giddings loved to get behind the counter and dish out food. Mr. Giddings always distinguished himself when he came because he did things that outraged people. But they loved it.

Once when he was stationed at the serving tray for rolls, a little old lady who was a fairly regular hotel guest was going through the line, and she asked for a roll. He gave her one. Then she said, "I would like another roll, please." T.P. said to her, "No, you can't have any more. You are fat enough anyway."

We had a lot of fun when T.P. was around.

Wendell and I went to Interlochen for one summer and stayed twenty-four. We raised our children there. They started as day campers when they were seven years old. When he grew up, our son John worked on the stage crew. Daughter Vickie taught ceramics on the art faculty, then married a young man whose father had been a conductor here. Interlochen was a great influence on our children.

104

Both still say that this is where they would like to live more than anyplace in the world.

We bought a little house on Long Lake, not far from Interlochen, and Wendell's grave is not far from Dr. Maddy's, on a little knoll in a cemetery near Traverse City. We have lifetime tickets to all the concerts, and each time I come out here the memories come rushing back. But one is most vivid. We had invited Dr. and Mrs. Maddy to go on a picnic with us on a Monday afternoon, Interlochen's only "day off" during the week. We went out to Point Betsy, that little piece of land the camp owns on Lake Michigan. Dr. Maddy told us how he had discovered it, through the Alice-in-Wonderland hole in the tangled arbors of grape vines.

He had a wonderful time at our picnic, and so did we. Wherever he went, he was living the music camp.

MINERVA TURNER is now retired and divides her time between Florida and Long Lake. She is still active in Interlochen events.

17
HELEN RICHTER
"I never thought we'd be innkeepers."

❧

My husband, Keith, was a violinist and director of instrumental music in the schools of Clayton, Missouri, a suburb
of St. Louis. I was a choir director and organist. Our daughter, Betty Jo, was in the fifth grade and just starting violin
lessons.

So of course we all knew about Interlochen and Dr.
Maddy. We had even thought of sending Betty Jo up there
to study when she was a little older and if we could
afford it.

One day in the summer of 1945 we got an urgent call
from a friend at the University of Michigan in Ann Arbor,
saying the camp was in desperate need of another counselor in the Boys' Camp. Would Keith be interested in the
job? He had never been a camp counselor, but he said,
"Why not?"

"When do you want me?" he asked.

"Tomorrow."

Dr. Joseph E. Maddy and Fay Maddy in front of the Interlochen Bowl Hotel

Dr. Maddy and John Philip Sousa, who came to the National Music Camp during the summers of 1930 and 1931. Sousa presented his "Northern Pines March" to Interlochen in 1931.

In 1931 Dr. Maddy turned his motor boat (named Largo Fortissimo *because it was slow and loud) into an aquaplane for Tex Payne.*

Dr. Maddy with Interlochen's disciplinarian, T. P. Giddings, in the early 1940s

T. P. Giddings testing students with his oscilloscope

Frederick Fennell playing vibraphone for the Blanket,
an Interlochen fund-raising tradition, in 1931

Conductor Howard Hanson of the
Eastman School of Music, about
1941

Dr. Maddy greeting Percy Grainger
at Interlochen's railroad station,
about 1944. Percy, known as the
camp "character," always carried a
knapsack on his back.

Russell Ogg and Dr. Maddy about 1944, with a nice catch of trout

Choral directors Ken Jewell (left) and Maynard Klein in 1954

George C. Wilson, former vice president and director of the National Music Camp

Dr. Joe Maddy: maker of no small plans

At his favorite fishing spot

With a young Van Cliburn

The Interlochen Bowl Hotel, 1945

Marcia Weissgerber Palmer with a violin student in the early 1940s

Trumpet player Nan Agricola, 1948

Interlochen "babies" Melinda and John Dalley. Their parents, Orien and Gretchen Dalley, met in the first National High School Orchestra and later became faculty members.

William D. Revelli, a well-known band conductor, with the High School Symphonic Band in 1969

Minerva and Wendell Turner, directors of Interlochen's cafeteria, about 1970

The violin section rehearsing by the lake in 1960

*Interlochen's dancers performed with the National High School Orchestra
at the White House in 1962 and met John F. Kennedy afterward.*

Norma Lee Browning and Joe Maddy signing copies of their 1963 book, Joe Maddy of Interlochen.

Van Cliburn conducts and Lucy Baines Johnson narrates a benefit performance of Peter and the Wolf *by the World Youth Symphony Orchestra in 1964.*

Bob Hope performing a benefit concert in 1975. He's backed up by Dave Sporny and the High School Stage Band.

Benny Goodman performing a benefit concert in 1975

Dedicated To The Promotion Of World Friendship Through The Universal Language Of The Arts

Conductor George Wilson introducing President Gerald and Betty Ford, who visited Interlochen in 1975

Interlochen president Roger Jacobi with President Ford during the Fords' 1975 visit

With the considerable help of W. Clement Stone, Dr. Maddy realized his dream of a year-round academy at Interlochen. (Photo by George Vincent)

The National High School Orchestra giving a concert in the Interlochen Bowl

He packed a bag and grabbed the first bus north. It was a twenty-four-hour trip.

The next summer all three of us went—Betty Jo as a camper, Keith and I as managers of the hotel. We had absolutely no knowledge of how to run a hotel. I had never even opened a cash register.

"Don't worry," Dr. Maddy said. "You can learn." He was so enthusiastic. You learn a lot of things besides music at Interlochen. We managed the hotel for twenty-one years. We didn't do it for the money. Nobody did. We worked our heads off like everyone else because we were devoted to Dr. Maddy and anxious to do anything we could to promote his dream.

I practically bowed and scraped to do everything he wanted me to do, though he didn't expect bowing and scraping. He always asked for things in such a nice, polite way that you *wanted* to do them. He was great at calling me and saying, "I have guests for this weekend," or "The Kresges are coming up—seven of them. I hope you can take care of them." I always said, "Sure," even if the hotel was full. I knew we would have cancellations.

The Kresge family gave the camp a great deal of money through the years, and they would have loved coming even if they had to sleep in the lobby, they said. Stanley Kresge always had to have a tennis game with Keith.

When Mr. and Mrs. Stone started coming up, they always stayed in the hotel. There weren't many guest cottages then. Later they stayed in the new Tremaine cottage down on the lake. But when they were in the hotel, they would get up about seven o'clock in the morning and always go down to the lake for their devotional period.

They would sit there on a bench, facing the lake, having their quiet time together before starting the day. I remember how touched I was by this, seeing them there together every morning, in the quiet time of the day before the hustle and bustle began. They seemed to be such a devoted couple. We became very fond of them.

They were always so pleasant, so quiet and gentle, and so extremely kind to everyone. I was surprised—and quite honored—when Mr. Stone presented me with an autographed copy of one of his books published in Australia. And he brought us cases of his books on Positive Mental Attitude to distribute to all our hotel guests—free!

Keith and I sometimes joked about our jobs. I never thought we'd be innkeepers. But we met some wonderful people, and Van Cliburn certainly was one of the tops. We were amazed, and I think everyone else was too, that with all his success and fame he could still be so modest and humble and so genuinely interested in working with the Interlochen students.

The first time Van came, there was a lot of excitement and suspense. He didn't arrive when he was supposed to. I took over the hotel switchboard, with Dr. Maddy right at my elbow, agitated and fidgeting, waiting for Van to call. He finally did. He was in Detroit. He had missed his plane to Traverse City. His parents had arrived the day before. I got them on the phone with Van, and they were telling him what nice people the Richters were and how he was going to meet some wonderful people at Interlochen. By this time, Dr. Maddy was jumping up and down. He could hardly stand it. He grabbed the phone and told Van to get a private plane and get up here. His rehearsal with the orchestra had been scheduled.

Van used Dr. Maddy's own don't-worry approach. He said it wasn't necessary to hire a private plane, he'd just take the next commercial flight, and he leisurely did.

He played his first benefit concert, and it was instant love between Van Cliburn and Interlochen. He came back for many summers. One summer he persuaded Lucy Baines Johnson, the U.S. president's daughter, to do *Peter and the Wolf* with Van conducting the high-school orchestra.

Barbara Walters was there, too, for an interview with Lucy Baines on the "Today" show. It was a hectic time at the hotel. Miss Walters wasn't enchanted with the hotel accommodations. We didn't have air conditioning. I took her a glass of iced tea and showed her how to put down wet towels and turn on the cold water in the shower to cool off the room.

Lucy Baines was calling her father in the White House three or four times a day, with people hovering over me wanting to listen in just so they could hear the president's voice on the phone. Before one of the rehearsals, Van discovered that Lucy Baines was missing, nowhere to be found, apparently off campus. We alerted her security guards. It wasn't necessary. One of them had spirited her off to see her boyfriend in Wisconsin. She got back with barely enough time for a rehearsal and pulled off *Peter and the Wolf* with somewhat more aplomb than talent. But, after all, she *was* the president's daughter.

It was a nice feather in Joe Maddy's cap even if he wasn't of the same political persuasion.

During all the years we were innkeepers at Interlochen, Keith continued his musical career. He played violin in the University Orchestra, took all the courses he could in the camp's University of Michigan extension program, handled the financial end of the hotel while I handled reservations, and played tennis with Stanley Kresge.

Betty Jo started in the Junior Girls division, finally made it up to third-chair violinist in the high-school orchestra, and got a position teaching music in elementary and junior high school in Midland, Michigan. Interlochen was a very important part of her life. It was for all of us.

HELEN RICHTER now lives in St. Louis, Missouri.

18
WAYNE BRILL

*"You always had a good feeling just knowing that Dr.
Maddy was around. You knew things were going to be all
right."*

❧

I came to Interlochen in the summer of 1955 for one
summer and stayed thirty-six years.

I am a photographer. I had my own photo studio in
Chicago and took time off in the summer of 1954 to be a
cabin counselor in a boys' camp at Lake Lelanau in northern Michigan, not far from Interlochen. Toward the end of
our camp season, all the boys and counselors were loaded
into buses for a special treat, an outing to Interlochen to
see a Gilbert and Sullivan operetta.

I didn't know Gilbert and Sullivan from borscht, but I
was swept off my feet by the enthusiasm of those kids. I
never saw anything like it. I didn't know anything about
Interlochen, and I didn't know Dr. Maddy. I had heard
about them, of course, but this was the first time I had ever
set foot on the place. I'll never forget it. There was something about it, especially the enthusiasm of the kids, that
just turned me on. I knew I had to come here.

I took a fast walk around the grounds, looking at the

111

buildings, peering through windows. Through the basement window of one building I saw some camera equipment and what appeared to be a photo lab. I hurried back to the ticket booth and asked the man in charge where or how I could apply for a job for the next summer. He told me where to pick up a job application.

The next summer I was back working in that photo lab as assistant to the camp photographer, Russell Ogg.

The enthusiasm of the kids never ceased to amaze me, and there was never any doubt in my mind about the reason for their enthusiasm: it was Dr. Maddy. Everything he did was for the kids. His influence was everywhere. I think the word *charisma* must have been invented especially for Dr. Maddy. He certainly had that special gift and talent for leadership that inspires unswerving allegiance and devotion.

He instilled his own confidence and enthusiasm in everyone else, not only the kids but everyone who worked for him. He made you feel important, no matter who you were. Not many men in his position would bother to introduce a staff photographer to a visiting VIP who was having his picture taken with him. Dr. Maddy always did. No matter how important the visitor was, Dr. Maddy always introduced us. He was very sensitive about things like that. And he didn't just say, "This is our photographer"; he would say, "This is Wayne Brill." That really makes you feel important when you're being introduced to someone like Van Cliburn!

Dr. Maddy had great faith and trust in the people he hired. He expected them to do their jobs. In the summer of 1962, on the way to Washington, D.C., to play a concert on the White House lawn for President Kennedy, the orchestra

112

stopped in Dearborn, Michigan. Rehearsal was scheduled to start in a few hours, and they were getting all set up when Peg Stace, who was his right arm, reported to Dr. Maddy that they couldn't find the music.

Dr. Maddy said, "Well, just find it. I'm not going to worry about it. I'm going to take a nap. That's the librarian's job, taking care of the music. Wake me up when they find it."

Everyone else was a little frantic and nervous. Not Dr. Maddy. He knew the music would be found. Of course it was, and the concert went off as scheduled.

I remember one time early in the camp season when we had some sort of a special event scheduled, and a prominent VIP—maybe a senator or someone like that— was coming. I knew we would need pictures of Dr. Maddy with the VIP. I caught Dr. Maddy on the run and asked whether he wanted any special kind of pictures taken. He stopped right where he was and said, "Now, Wayne, you're the photographer, you figure it out. That's your job; that's what we pay you for. Just go ahead and do what you think is right. Don't worry about it. Everything will be all right."

At concerts everybody would look to see where Dr. Maddy was sitting. It was important to know where he was sitting, important to see him around—at rehearsals, in and out of classes, everywhere. You always had a good feeling just knowing that Dr. Maddy was around. He inspired such a feeling of trust. You knew things were going to be all right.

WAYNE AND MARY BRILL are a well-known husband-and-wife photo team in the Grand Traverse area and live near Interlochen.

19
MARGUERITTE HOUSE
"I'm the one responsible for the knickers."

❧

I'm a musician. I guess everyone here is. I was first cellist in the Chicago Symphony when I was offered the job of director of the Girls' Camp.

The first thing Dr. Maddy said to me was, "People say we can't have a camp up here in the woods for both boys and girls without moral problems. It is your job to see that nothing happens."

The place was rather primitive. There were no blankets for the beds. They had pillows and sheets but no blankets. So I went into Traverse City and bought some army blankets.

In the early years there were only thirteen girls, compared with a hundred boys. Parents just didn't send their girls into the woods without knowing what was going on. These girls would practice like fiends, mostly because Dr. Maddy started them in on the challenges right away. I felt the girls needed to get away from their instruments for a while, so we would have picnics and cookouts every now and then.

I'm the one responsible for the knickers. The students had been wearing khaki uniforms, and they looked terrible. So I suggested blue corduroy knickers for the girls and slacks for the boys, with a blue shirt for weekdays, white shirt for Sunday. I had to have the knickers made. I dressed up a pretty little blonde girl in the outfit to show off my idea. The counselors liked it. Dr. Maddy liked it. (That was most important.) But I had no idea it would last this long. Even though they are a bit outdated, they are very practical. I've been kidded a lot about starting this business.

When I first arrived in my cabin, I noticed an old-fashioned bowl and pitcher. I mean really old-fashioned. The pitcher didn't even have a handle. I said, "What's that doing here?" I knew there was running water in the cottage—I think we had hot water but I'm not sure. It wouldn't have made any difference to me anyway. I was intrigued by that pitcher and bowl. I found out they were gifts from Henry Ford. He had outfitted a peace ship to send to Europe before World War I. Dr. Maddy had asked him for a donation to the camp. This was not in keeping with Henry Ford's philosophy. He said, "I don't believe in giving money to any institution that isn't halfway self-supporting. But I'll tell you what I'll do. I'll give you some things off my peace ship."

So he gave the washbowls and pitchers and a bunch of lanterns that are still in the Bowl.

I remember many things about those early days—the times when John Philip Sousa came and the Bowl was overfilled and people sat on the ground on the hillside . . .

115

and Sousa outdid himself. He would raise his baton and order the downbeat, and those kids were playing like angels. . . .

Then there was Percy Grainger. I watched him leap like a kangaroo over those benches down at the Bowl, one after another. People told me I looked like Percy Grainger. I went into his studio one day after he had finished teaching and I said, "Mr. Grainger, I'm told I look like you and I hope you are not insulted."

He said, "Turn around." He looked at me and said, "Yes, you do."

But mostly I remember Dr. Maddy and the way he was always doing what people said was impossible. He was always looking over the mountain to the next crest. He never paid any attention to money when he was spending it. He just expected things to happen, and they did. He kept digging these holes, and then he would fill them up when he got the money. A lot of people laughed at him then. But not now.

MARGUERITTE HOUSE was dean of girls at the first National Music Camp season in 1928 and returned each summer as a staff member in various capacities until her death in 1979. She taught music in Tulsa and later became associate professor of music at Florida State University. This interview was conducted in 1975.

20
Marie Dorothy "Pete" Hartwig

*"When we asked for new things, he would say, 'Why not?
If it doesn't work we'll stop it.' He never said no, but we
didn't ask for the moon."*

❧

My first year as director of recreation at Interlochen was
1944. I was assistant athletic director in charge of women's
intercollegiate at the University of Michigan. I didn't want
to come here, because I loved teaching in Ann Arbor. But
I came and I loved it, and I have been here ever since.

One of the reasons I was impressed with the camp was
because Dr. Maddy was so willing to try new ideas. I would
ask him if we could try this or that, and he would say,
"Why not? If it doesn't work we'll stop it." He never said
"no." We never asked him for the moon or anything silly.
What we asked for was something that would be an attrib-
ute to the program, and he took us at our word. If we didn't
deliver the goods, then it was stopped.

Dr. Maddy was a very ingenious man who also taught
you to be ingenious. He was always full of enthusiasm and
excited about something. It was like he was walking down
a road and if there was a fence blocking his way, he would
turn and go in another direction to get around it.

I remember going with Dr. Maddy and three counselors to Point Betsy to look at some property. We got in the car. I'm sure it didn't have any brakes. Dr. Maddy was driving, of course, and I remember going down a big hill with railroad tracks at the bottom. I wondered what would happen if a train came along.

Finally he parked the car, and we followed him like little children. He took us down into a great big dell, sort of, a green forest with dunes around it. Then he said, "Now, I'll walk along down here and you all go on up there. I want you to see the view from that ridge." Well, it was like walking straight up the side of a wall, but we made it up there. The view just took your breath away. We walked along the ridge and looked down and saw the tops of the trees below us, and he was down there among those trees, hollering all sorts of things for us to look at from up there. Pretty soon he yelled, "Now, stop right there and come down."

I yelled back at him, "Down *here?*" He shouted, "Yes!" This time it was like coming down the side of a wall. Well, we got down to the forest floor and into an enormous mass of grape vines. I was sure no human beings had ever walked in there, except Indians maybe. We had to help one another over fallen trees and rocks and those vines. We scrambled on and finally came to an opening, kind of a big hole with a view framed in grape leaves. I felt like Alice in Wonderland looking through that hole and out onto a wide expanse of sand and then the blue of Lake Michigan blending with the blue sky.

Dr. Maddy said, "I just wanted you to see it now, the way it is. I want the kids to have their first glimpse of Lake Michigan from this place here. We could bring the trucks in

and open up a road, a circle around those trees over there."
I couldn't see how, but *he* could. His hands were flying in
all directions as he talked. "We could unload the kids over
there and build a path through the forest, and they could
go out to the beach from here.

"Those kids work hard. They need recreation. There's
no reason on earth why any child shouldn't have some free
time on that beach in the sun."

No matter that the kids already had their own smaller
lakes with beaches, Lake Wahbekanetta for the girls, Lake
Wahbekaness for boys (half a mile apart). Dr. Maddy
wanted them to have this special piece of Lake Michigan
with its glorious entrance and view.

"I'm going to buy this property," he said.

And he did. I don't know where he got the money.

He was a man of great vision and foresight.

MARIE DOROTHY ("PETE") HARTWIG lives in
Ann Arbor, Michigan, and was recently honored by the
University of Michigan by having a building named after
her.

21
ANNE HELLIER

*"He opened musical doors for me that I had never
imagined existed."*

❧

When I hear Schubert's *Unfinished Symphony* now, it just
doesn't sound right, because for me it can never measure
up to the memory of that first time I heard it and played it
in a marble palace with Dr. Maddy conducting.

It wasn't really a palace—it was a bank building in
Detroit in the early 1940s. But it was all marble: marble
floors, marble walls, huge marble columns. You can imagine how those acoustics impressed a high-school student
playing first viola in a symphony orchestra for the first
time.

Between his summers at Interlochen, Dr. Maddy spent
most of his time traveling, trying to raise money, and often
conducting orchestras to promote his music camp. He
came to work a while directing the Northwest Detroit Symphony Orchestra and the Plymouth (Michigan) Symphony.
Both of these orchestras disappeared into World War II, but
in those few short months he was here Dr. Maddy opened
musical doors to me that I had never imagined existed.

He made serious music a rich and lasting experience

that went beyond hunting for correct notes. He showed us how to hear the blend of the composer's work and how our individual contribution enriched the whole.

This was important for my viola. I was not just the first-chair viola. I was a full partner in producing the voice of his orchestra. The viola was no longer merely the two-three beat in a waltz. It was an integral part of an orchestra, as much a factor in the richness of the sound of the whole orchestral voice as any other instrument. I never realized this until Dr. Maddy taught us, showed us how our own individual instruments fit in to make music like this. You could see and feel him listening, working, trying to help all of us make the best contribution we could.

I was never a student at Interlochen. I could not accept a scholarship offered me. I had to give up my viola because of polio, which left me with an arm unable to control the bow. But I was able to transfer what I learned from Dr. Maddy to singing in various choruses with those wonderful choral directors, Kenneth Jewell and Maynard Klein. Dr. Maddy gave me the courage and confidence to sing with them in their choruses in Detroit.

Fate has a strange way of steering your life in unexpected directions. By happenstance I now live on a little ranch only a few lakes away and across the woods from Interlochen. I go there for concerts. But the music is always the same in my memory: the rich sound of Schubert's *Unfinished Symphony* in my childhood's marble palace. Dr. Maddy made *Interlochen* a magic word. His dream is unfinished, too, but, like Schubert's symphony, it lives on.

ANN HELLIER is now retired and lives on a ranch near Interlochen, where she raises bees.

121

22
ORIEN DALLEY

"To him nothing was impossible—even shaving John Philip
Sousa's beard."

❧

I was with Joe Maddy from the beginning of his dream in
the early twenties. I helped in organizing and promoting
his first National High School Orchestra, an enormous task.
I was with him in Detroit in 1926 for that memorable
concert when nobody believed such young people could
play music like that. Nobody except Joe Maddy and T. P.
Giddings.

Ossip Gabrilowitsch, the great Russian pianist, was the
conductor of the Detroit Symphony. He had married Mark
Twain's daughter and was on his way to American citizen-
ship. Victor Kolar was his assistant. The time for the first
rehearsal arrived. It was hectic—the stage was over-
crowded and there were not enough chairs and stands.
Gabrilowitsch had been asked to conduct a Tchaikovsky
symphony. This was his reply: "I travel the world over to
find a concertmaster, a first oboe, bassoon, or horn. No,
certainly these children cannot play Tchaikovsky."

Victor Kolar was in the hall at the third day's rehearsal

when the orchestra was playing the Tchaikovsky symphony. He leaned forward in his seat, then stood up and hurriedly left to see the maestro. On arriving he said to him, "Mr. Gabrilowitsch, a modern miracle has taken place. They can play Tchaikovsky." Ossip Gabrilowitsch conducted the historic event.

An all-orchestra camp was to open in June of 1928. Joe Maddy had no capital. It was a mammoth undertaking to prepare a place for some two hundred high-school orchestra players in the facilities used by lumberjacks and fishermen. The rustic, rambling lumber hotel would be the pivotal building where all the students would eat and where the camp offices would begin operations. It would also house all guests and some faculty, with the remaining families living in the half dozen fishing cabins.

An outdoor facility, the Bowl, was a must, as were the student cabins. The Bowl was located close to the lake in a low area, which had been used as a dump.

On June 25, at our first regular rehearsal, we played the entire *New World Symphony*, the *Rienzi* Overture and the *L'Arlésienne* Suite no. 2. It all went well, with the exception of the third movement of the symphony, which was terrible.

Joe Maddy's approach to music pedagogy was not traditional. He believed that a student learned more by doing and playing great music than by plugging away on scales and exercises. He believed in friendly competition at all levels, and he was opposed to placement based on age or experience. He and T. P. Giddings instituted the weekly tryout and challenge system, which has proved to be one of Interlochen's greatest contributions to music education. It produced startling results.

Many professional teachers and conductors contended that his plan of performing a major program each week was impossible. They wanted to perform only one program in the entire eight weeks.

John Philip Sousa was one of the most popular performers and conductors in America during his long and eventful life. At Interlochen he always drew huge crowds. During one of his last visits there, shortly after he had had a slight concussion, Dr. Maddy asked me to look after him at night and to shave him. He was famous for his heavy beard covering, and all I had to remove it with was a Gillette razor scraper.

During one of these ordeals he told me how he had won the First World War. One morning, he related, during one of his customary walks, he accosted a lone military man. When the man saw Sousa and his heavy beard, he turned livid with rage, about-faced, and disappeared.

Several days later Sousa encountered the stranger again, and he reacted more violently than before. Later that morning a messenger came bearing a message: "Shave off your beard and the war is over." It was signed "Bill (the Kaiser)."

ORIEN DALLEY and his wife, Gretchen, a cellist from Bloomington, Illinois, first met in Joe Maddy's National High School Orchestra in Dallas in 1927. Both worked for the music camp from its beginning. Their children, John and Melinda Dalley, grew up at Interlochen from infancy and became prominent professional musicians.

23
Don Th. Jaeger

"If you happened to be standing in the wrong place when he had an idea, you'd get a job."

❧

I first came to Interlochen in 1953, when I was seventeen years old. I was from Ponca City, Oklahoma, and played oboe in the Tri-State Music Festival in Enid, Oklahoma. This was an orchestra with players from all over the Midwest. Dr. Maddy had come there to hear us and to recruit students for his orchestra at Interlochen. I received a Tri-State scholarship to Interlochen. It changed my life.

I was a student for many years and worked at many odd jobs. I ran the program office, drove a station wagon, taught oboe. I was young and enthusiastic. When I left Interlochen, I accepted Clyde Roller's invitation to join the Amarillo (Texas) Symphony. He was the conductor. He was also a conductor at Interlochen in the summers.

In Amarillo, we formed a woodwinds quintet that became pretty well known. In February of 1962, the Amarillo Woodwinds Quintet was playing a concert at the Texas Music Educators' conference. When it was over, I got a message from an Interlochen official that Dr. Maddy wanted to talk to me. He wanted to know if I would be interested in teaching oboe at his new Arts Academy, which was opening in the fall.

The next day I got a call from Dr. Maddy from Interlochen, at six o'clock in the morning—he'd forgotten the time difference—saying he wanted to tell me personally, he needed an oboe teacher for his new Arts Academy and he wanted me there.

I was happy with the Amarillo Symphony. I told him I couldn't desert Clyde Roller and our winds quintet. The next day I got another call from Dr. Maddy. He said, "We need a winds faculty. Why don't you come and bring the whole quintet?"

That's what we did after talking it over with Clyde Roller. He was negotiating to go to Eastman anyway. But he loved Interlochen and Dr. Maddy. He was Joe Maddy's first choice to be his successor, and they talked about it many times. But Clyde Roller was a conductor. He loved conducting and he wanted no part of administrative details. However, he encouraged all of us in the quintet to go back to Interlochen and teach at the new Arts Academy.

We were all former students: Melinda Dalley, bassoon and cello; Fred Ormond, clarinet; Ramona Dahlborg, flute; John Reed, French horn; and myself, oboe. We all had had our youthful indoctrination in Joe Maddy's National Music Camp. We were returning as the first charter members of his faculty for that dream of his which everyone else thought was crazy: a year-round school, his Arts Academy.

I wasn't there long before I learned there were other jobs for me besides teaching oboe. If you happened to be standing in the wrong place when he got an idea, you'd get a job, whether you knew how to do it or not. He always had so many ideas going at one time, he couldn't do them all himself. He needed someone to take them over. If you happened to be standing in the wrong place, he'd drop them in your lap and ask you to do them.

During my first year of teaching at the Academy, there was an NBC music program called "The Best of Interlochen." It was narrated by Ben Grauer, then a well-known radio personality, and the program was very successful. This is how it happened.

One day Dr. Maddy stopped me on the steps of the Maddy Administration Building and said, "Don, I've got an idea. We're going to do a radio show from Interlochen, and I need somebody to select the music and write the scripts."

I'd never written a radio script in my life. But I did then. I wrote all the scripts and selected the music for Ben Grauer's program, "The Best of Interlochen."

During my second year at the Academy, Dr. Maddy tapped me on the shoulder and said, "I need someone to conduct the Interlochen Arts Academy Band." It was brand new—and so was I at conducting. Like many musicians, I was interested in conducting but I'd had no experience.

I learned and the experience served me well. I'm a conductor today because I happened to be standing in the wrong place when Joe Maddy had an idea and needed a job done.

People ask me all the time about my name, the Don *Th*. Jaeger. Clyde Roller was responsible for that. When I finally became interested in seriously pursuing a career as a conductor, Clyde said, "Don, you've got everything against you. You don't have long hair. You don't have a foreign accent. And you're from Texas and Oklahoma. All those things are against you. You need a *thing*, something to distinguish you, a trademark."

I had lived in Holland while on a Fulbright scholarship, and I noticed that the Dutch abbreviated the name Theodore—my middle name—to *Th*. So I borrowed it. Only I always tell people it stands for *"Thing"* because that's what Clyde Roller called it.

It really has worked very well. I conducted a concert once with Phyllis Diller as guest artist—she's a superb pianist—and the audience nearly cracked up with her guttural rendition of *Thhhhhh*.

DON TH. JAEGER is musical director and conductor of the Midland-Odessa Symphony in Texas and the Northwood Orchestra for its Festival of the Lakes concerts in northern Michigan during summers. He and his wife, Ann, a Spanish teacher, met at Interlochen when they were charter members of the Arts Academy faculty in 1962. Their two children, Jon and Julie, were "Interlochen babies" and are now successful in their own arts careers. Jaeger is also well known in the music world as a conductor of Bach festivals.

24
DOROTHY KUNKEL

"He always had time for the smallest child."

❧

I came from Weeping Water, Nebraska, a very small town, only a thousand in population when everybody's home. I played flute and piccolo and violin in the Weeping Water Little Symphony, which my father conducted. He was the town's physician, musician, and violin maker. I also played in the school band, which was awful.

When I came to Interlochen, I brought the cowgirl hat and boots which I wore in Weeping Water. But they didn't belong with knickers.

I'd heard about Interlochen and thought it would be Utopia. When the train pulled in, it was in the middle of a cornfield or something. I can still remember getting off the train, kids and baggage everywhere. I couldn't see a depot. I thought to myself, "This is Interlochen?"

I was on a career borderline between music and medicine. After two days I knew. I had never played in a real symphony orchestra before. I had never known the thrill of making beautiful music. It was like falling in love. I fell completely in love with Interlochen and music. From that point on there was no question in my mind about what I wanted to do.

Dr. Maddy was one of those people who knew everybody. He had a genuine knack for making you feel that he cared about you, and he wanted you to know it. He was very busy, but he always had time for kids, even for the smallest child. That made a big impression on me.

But in my mind the most outstanding thing about him was that he didn't know the meaning of the word *no*, especially when it came to getting things done or going ahead. He only knew how to say no when something was wrong.

He was a person of action. His energy was amazing. One thing that really astounded me the first time I saw him do it—and it still amazes me every time I think about it—he could stand on the podium and have five different rhythms going at the same time. He could tap a different rhythm with each foot, conduct two other rhythms with each hand, and talk a fifth one. I remember him doing that. We just couldn't believe it. Any person who can do that really has an organized mind.

One summer he switched all violin players to viola for a week. We always were short on violas, and this was his way of rounding out the viola section in the orchestra—just take a violinist a week at a time and put him or her in the viola section. I had never played viola in my life. The instruments look alike, but they're not. They are in a different class, though three of the strings are the same. Dr. Maddy said it's very simple for a violinist to switch to viola—you just play in third position and add the sharps and flats. So I decided if he said I could do it that way, then it must be right, and that's what I did.

I remember how sad I felt at the end of my first summer at camp. The standards set by Dr. Maddy and his spirit and enthusiasm left an indelible impression on me. I was like a sponge because I had never had anything like this in my whole life. In Weeping Water we had maybe a twenty-five-piece awful band, and of course my parents and I played good music, but it wasn't a symphonic sound. I was going back to just nowhere musically. I knew it was going to be difficult.

I still remember Dr. Maddy's speech to us at the honors assembly on that last Sunday at camp. He said, "We have had a wonderful summer. You have played Brahms and Beethoven and Tchaikovsky, and some of you are going back to places that might have comparable music to play and hear. But for many of you this has been a highlight in your life that you will never experience again unless you come back here.

"I hope that all of you will go back, no matter where it is, and try to make a real contribution to whatever group you play in. Don't feel that any group is not good enough to play with. You can make your personal contribution by trying to pull the others up to your level, instead of thinking you're too good to play with them."

There were many times during the coming school year at home when I didn't really want to go to a band rehearsal at eight o'clock in the morning and play things that I could play in my sleep. But then I would remember Dr. Maddy's words, and I knew that I had a contribution to make and that I should go and try to make the group a little better in my own way.

I also made an important decision. I was going to go back to Interlochen and become a conductor. I always knew I wanted to be like my father—either a doctor or a musician and conductor. It was Dr. Maddy who unknowingly made the decision for me.

I studied conducting with Clyde Roller. He is a great conductor and wonderful with young people. He really inspired me and encouraged me to go into conducting professionally, even though women conductors were, and still are, rather rare. I don't think it makes any difference whether you are a woman or a man. To be good, you just have to know what you are doing. I've done a lot of guest conducting in the Midwest. I've never had any doors shut on me that I know of.

I was at Interlochen three summers as a student. This is my sixth summer here as a faculty member, as a conductor and teacher of conducting classes.

I think maybe I had a special rapport with Dr. Maddy because he was originally from a small town in Kansas— Wellington—and I was from Weeping Water, Nebraska. I can remember that we talked about the Midwest a lot. He had a sense of humor. He liked the cowgirl outfits I wore for publicity pictures. But when the photo session ended, it was back into knickers and knee socks.

DOROTHY KUNKEL became one of the best-known women conductors in the Midwest and spent several years as a conductor in the Chicago area before tiring of city life and moving back to northern Michigan. She now conducts the Traverse City High School Orchestra and teaches music and conducting classes. This interview was conducted in 1975.

25
HOMER KELLER

"Anything could happen here. The sky was the limit."

🌿

Dr. Maddy doesn't know it, but he shaped my destiny.

I was a farm boy, just graduated from high school in Oxnard, California, in 1933, and I was driving up the coast near Santa Barbara, in a little old Model A Ford, wondering where I was going to get a job and what I was going to do with my life.

I turned on the car radio and an NBC announcer said, "This is music from Interlochen . . . Dr. Joseph E. Maddy conducting Howard Hanson's *Romantic Symphony. . . .*"

I had never heard of Interlochen, Joe Maddy, or Howard Hanson, but by the time the music was finished, I knew where I was going. To Interlochen. It took me a while to get there. I went to Eastman first to study with Howard Hanson. I had graduated and was teaching composition and theory at the University of Michigan when Dr. Maddy came to Ann Arbor looking for people to help expand his music camp program.

Those first few summers I was one of the elite, with a

professor's salary from the University of Michigan. I taught in the camp's University Extension division. Later, when I joined the faculty of the University of Oregon, it was a different story. Usually I had to take three or four hundred dollars out of my savings to come to Interlochen during summers. But it was worth it.

No one comes here for monetary reasons.

I came here for the challenge of teaching composition, especially to the younger students. Most of my teaching had been at the university level. But I found there was a real reward and thrill in teaching these youngsters in their formative High School and Junior and Intermediate years.

Composition classes were comparatively new at Interlochen then. It was a period when Dr. Maddy was becoming more interested in developing the creative talents of his students. His theory was—get them started early—the earlier, the better. Encourage them by giving more work to do in the actual writing of music, composing.

He was always finding new ways of making things happen. Innovation and experimenting were a way of life at Interlochen. He never gave me specific instructions. He just said, "That's your field—composition. Do what you find exciting."

He gave you the feeling that anything could happen here. The sky was the limit. He liked to show off his composition classes. He was always dropping by with visitors. He didn't come in and sit down—he never interrupted classes. But if he was interested in something we were discussing, he would stay a few minutes and then leave. He was always on the go, always encouraging, always interested in how the students were progressing.

And we were always delighted to see that familiar head

around the corner, for there would be Dr. Maddy and some visitors. I often thought how lucky these kids were to have someone like that so concerned and interested.

What I would have given for someone like that when I was their age! Instead, I was down on the farm with no exposure to music except by radio and a few piano lessons.

One of my earliest impressions of Dr. Maddy was how involved and enthusiastic he was with his students. From the moment I first set eyes on the man, I knew why he was such a success. He was up there on the podium, in action, conducting a rehearsal. There was such kindness, such gentleness, even tenderness in the way he handled those kids. You could tell he really loved them, and the way they responded was like magic. It was marvelous to watch, a warm and wonderful experience for me. I had never before nor since seen such a rapt, special rapport between any group of musicians and a conductor.

At the end of the rehearsal, he thanked them, told them what a wonderful job they had done, and then as he was leaving the stage he sort of swept up some of the string players and said exuberantly, "Come on down to my cabin, and we'll play some string quartets together."

I was dumbfounded. And even more so when he turned to me and said, "You come along, too."

I had just been sitting there watching. I was awed, I was new, and I tended at the time to be a little shy. I think he sensed this. I was reluctant to go. I told him I didn't play any string instrument.

"That's all right," he said, gently grabbing my arm and tugging me along. "You don't need to play. You can just sit there and watch. Maybe you'll learn something."

I did. I learned that here was a man whose magic

135

could turn on rainbows in a child's eyes and floods of joy in a child's heart.

For two hours I sat there watching Dr. Maddy and his students playing string quartets together. Mrs. Maddy came out with her knitting and joined me. She was very friendly and made me feel so comfortable and welcome. Afterward, she served us milk and her homemade cookies.

The memory of that day is locked in my mind like a time warp. The afterglow will never fade. The glorious music, the rapture on those young faces, the shimmering lake in the sunset, the peaceful harmony of it all. . . . For one splendid, shining moment in time, I knew that all was right with the world.

HOMER KELLER is now retired and lives on a farm in Oregon.

26
DICK MADDY

"I didn't get away with anything because I was Dick Maddy."

❧

My earliest memory of my father is when he put the violin in my hands. I was still in a crib, but I remember it vividly. He put this huge instrument in the bed with me and let me touch it. He even handed me the bow, but not for very long. Later he told me it was a quarter-size violin. It was as big as I was. He also used to play the clarinet for us—crescendos and other special effects that he used to play in jazz concerts with Isham Jones.

The first instrument he gave me lessons on was the clarinet. I then started to play the baritone horn. I didn't like that too much, so when I was eleven I got a pair of drumsticks. I was never much of a string player. I was eight or nine years old when I started the clarinet.

I think his ability to find people to do the job right and leave them alone to do it was very important. He used to say to me, "A smart executive gets someone to do it better than he can." He never thought that anything he tried was impossible.

My first memory of the camp was when they were putting the floors and cement pilings in the cabins. I remember thinking something was wrong when I saw a toilet sitting out in the open with no walls. I think it was one of those things Henry Ford gave us from his peace ship. That was about 1927.

Dad walked and talked fast. One time he wrote me a note to do something and put it on my desk. I couldn't read a word of it, it had been written so fast. When he came back I asked him to please translate it. He just looked at it and laughed. He couldn't read it either. I framed it and put it on the wall.

Dad was ruthless in a good way. I didn't get away with anything just because I was Dick Maddy. He held me responsible for a lot of things.

It was never dull to be around him. He was always interesting. The times I found him the dullest was when he was playing. He was having a good time, but when he wasn't playing, he was talking. I still dream about him, and I wish he were here. I can't recall a time when I didn't want to be around him.

If I could do anything I wanted to or dreamed about, I would be making violins. I think I have more to give than I have been able to give.

This interview with Dick Maddy was taped in the summer of 1975. On August 8, 1991, preceding a "Welcome Back, Mr. Sousa" concert in the Interlochen Bowl, Dick Maddy paid a moving tribute to his father and to Mr. and Mrs. W. Clement Stone. "I do not think my father would mind if I say they are truly the founders of the Interlochen Arts Academy," he said.

138

He recalled, "After a year of combat, I was released from an army hospital and allowed to come home for Christmas 1944. Dad said 'Merry Christmas' and gave me a watch engraved 'To Dick from Dad.' We didn't talk about the war. Guess what we discussed. Within five minutes my father said, 'We're going to have a winter school at Interlochen.' This was in 1944. I don't know how long before that he'd been thinking about it. Then he said, 'And we have a *real* violin maker at camp. If you don't want to play the violin, then maybe you can learn to make one.' "

He did. Today Dick Maddy is known as a master craftsman violin maker, one of the few left in that rarefied world of arts skills. During summers he works as a violin maker and head of violin repairs for the National Music Camp. The rest of the year he does a thriving and successful business making violins. Though his son never learned to play the violin—or the clarinet or the drums—his father would be proud of him.

"So nobody could invent another Joe Maddy," Dick Maddy says philosophically. "But my dream is to keep his spirit alive."

27
MAYNARD KLEIN

"He's a wholesome fanatic. . . . There's something electric about the place. You don't just sit around and drink mint juleps."

༝

I had known Joe Maddy from his early years in Ann Arbor, where he was supervisor of music in the public schools, which was really fertile territory for him. When he arrived, the only instrumental music in the entire high-school system was a mandolin club!

He was expected to produce a music program as fine as the one he had developed in Richmond, Indiana, but with far fewer natural resources and far more resistance to giving school credits for music. Even the state's own prestigious University of Michigan in Ann Arbor did not then accept music credits toward entrance. Consequently, high-school teachers generally advised their students not to take music—or ordered them to drop band and orchestra and spend more time on their Latin and mathematics.

Dr. Maddy lost three of four horn players the first month. Nevertheless, he managed to develop a band and orchestra that won honorable mention at the state contest the following spring. He also organized a marching band

140

for football games and persuaded the Ann Arbor Rotary Club to donate two thousand dollars for its uniforms.

In his early years in Ann Arbor he made several innovations that neither he nor anyone else—as far as is known—had ever tried before. One was a conducting class in the university's school of music—though Joe Maddy himself had had only one lesson in conducting. That one lesson was from Albert Coates of the Rochester (New York) Philharmonic Orchestra and former conductor of the London Symphony, and Joe Maddy remembered it well: Coates had simply pointed to a symphony score, Tchaikovsky's Sixth, and said, "The way to conduct is to learn your score. Then *lead*, don't follow." That was all.

Dr. Maddy started his class in conducting by having members of his orchestra sign up for it. This way he got both his conducting class and an orchestra for the class to conduct. All students brought their instruments to the conducting class and took turns leading the group. All players were instructed not to play unless the student-player-conductor was actually *leading*. As players, they were used to following along with the group; and as Dr. Maddy himself had once learned, the transition from following to leading was not easy. Nevertheless, within a year Dr. Maddy had a number of fine student conductors among his orchestra members—as well as fine orchestra players in his conducting class. Many later became conductors of university bands and orchestras. And every member of that class achieved success as a music educator.

Another of his innovations was music lessons by radio. This was long before educational programs on radio and television came into vogue. The university's director of broadcasting had first asked him to give lessons in music

141

appreciation by radio. Dr. Maddy asked if he could give music-playing lessons instead. The director was startled, but he apparently decided that if Joe Maddy wanted to risk his reputation because of a public failure on the air, that was his privilege. If it proved to be embarrassing to the university, the program could be eliminated.

But the program was a success that exceeded even Joe Maddy's dreams. In three years he had radio classes in more than a thousand towns in Michigan, and by 1937 he was presenting weekly radio lessons over NBC's coast-to-coast network to an invisible class estimated at more than 225,000 pupils scattered from New Zealand to Persia.

All of his pioneering in music lessons by radio had to be dropped before long, however, because of the ban imposed by James C. Petrillo, then president of the Chicago Federation of Musicians and well known as the Czar of Music. Petrillo objected to the radio music lessons because they were training musicians to compete with "his boys," union members. No radio pupil was permitted to play over the air and no visitor was allowed in the studio under any circumstances.

He later banned all "Music from Interlochen" concerts and all union members from setting foot on the grounds of the National Music Camp. His aim was to destroy the music camp because it was "taking the bread out of the mouths" of his union musicians.

With one swift bombshell, he eliminated the music camp faculty, most of whom were professional conductors and thus union members. But with one swift coup, Joe Maddy recruited in two months enough nonunion music educators to help him open a summer music camp that

Petrillo thought would never be able to open again. All during his early years in Ann Arbor, in the thirties, Maddy was struggling to make his summer music camp go—he was traveling around the state promoting it and trying to get students. His salary from the University of Michigan was three thousand dollars per year. Mr. Petrillo's income was then listed at twenty-five thousand a year.

No one but a man with the guts of Joe Maddy would take on a man like that. Interlochen was banned from the airwaves and union musicians were forbidden to play or teach there, but in the end Joe Maddy won. Petrillo turned out to be Maddy's greatest press agent. All the press and communications media aligned themselves with this little guy from a little place called Interlochen who dared to battle a big union bozo like Petrillo. It was great publicity for Interlochen. The National Music Camp not only survived but thrived.

I have always felt very much a part of Joe Maddy's life because I was there during some of those early years in Ann Arbor. I was working on my master's degree in the university's School of Music and was a member of Joe Maddy's conducting class.

I spent the summer of 1938 as a student at Interlochen, in the University division. As I recall, my future then didn't look too promising with all those other talented young people.

But when I finished my graduate work at the University of Michigan, I was offered a position as choral director at Tulane University in New Orleans, and then, lo and behold, Dr. Maddy called and asked me to be choral director at Interlochen.

143

I couldn't wait. It was the summer of 1943. I had a wife and two small children. We packed our bags, drove to Interlochen, put our kids in camp, and moved into H-1 on Faculty Row with the bats. It was marvelous.

I worked with Dr. Maddy until he died and saw him turn his frustrations into positive activity. He never followed the usual business or educational pattern. He was completely an individual. He would build a million-dollar camp with five cents and develop a style of teaching that everyone said couldn't be done. He would hire subordinates and give them completely free rein. In all the time I worked for him I was never held back.

He didn't operate like a businessman, yet he built up a big business. Some musicians said he couldn't conduct, but he did conduct and organize the finest group of young symphony orchestras in the world. Some music educators have laughed at his ideas. But then they went out and adopted them as their own.

To my mind, Joe Maddy was a wholesome fanatic, an extremely wholesome rebel who rebelled against conformity, complacency, and laziness. In his mind there was no salvation for the man who would not work. He used that word *work* all the time: "*work* scholarships," "this is a *work* camp, not a play camp," and so on.

Sometimes I wondered what I was doing there working a ninety-hour week when I could be home fishing and drinking mint juleps. But there's something electrifying about four hundred young voices singing the *Berlioz Requiem* in a festival choir.

And, besides, how do you say no to a man like Joe Maddy?

MAYNARD KLEIN retired and lived in Ann Arbor but continued to come to Interlochen as guest conductor until his death in 1990. These interviews were conducted during the 1960s and in 1975.

28
KEN JEWELL

*"Once you are here and get the feel for it, you are never
the same again."*

❧

I came here in 1949 as a piano tuner and a choral director.
I was supposed to be retired from the music business. I
found out I wasn't. My wife, Mary, came with me, and we
put our three kids in camp.

At the end of the summer after we paid all our bills, we
had fifty cents left. We blew it on ice-cream cones.

We were shocked when we saw those old houses,
where we had to live. But it was the same for everyone. So
we made jokes about it and it was fun. We called the area
Skunk Hollow. Either you are an Interlochen person or you
are not.

I had met Dr. Maddy a few years earlier in Ann Arbor,
only briefly. He was always on the lookout for people he
needed at camp. He asked, "What do you do?" I told him I
was a choral director and I could tune pianos.

"Well, we need a piano tuner," he said. So he hired me
on the spot, and I've been there ever since as a piano tuner
and a choral director. I don't know why I waited thirty

years to go to Interlochen. It changed our lives, as it has many others. Our children grew up here. They absorbed everything they learned from this place, mostly from Joe Maddy. Eventually they all became professional musicians. One of them, a violinist, ended up on the faculty.

Mary and I were in high school together, and we both sang. We were in the school choir, the church choir, any choir we could find. I went on and got my master's degree and became a teacher and choral director in Detroit. When we came to Interlochen, Mary sang in my choir and Dr. Maddy put her to work in the attendance office. Everybody had to do something. It was really a work camp.

But you had the feeling that you *wanted* to help this great man. You were compelled to do it. He had a very compelling personality. He also had a nervous habit of brushing his bushy eyebrows, which usually meant he was impatient to get on with whatever he was doing or wanted you to do. It was so characteristic of him, the gesture of brushing his eyebrows, and it made us all want to help this impatient man.

He never gave me any instructions when I started, at least not verbally. But I got the message: Just do it, and do it now. He had great faith in people and a great kindness toward them, but nothing ever got in the way of his camp or the Academy. You could see this from his disciplinary actions. Many people disagreed with some of them, but the discipline sure helped him run a tight ship.

A lot of people thought he would never be able to run a summer camp for both boys and girls, a co-ed camp in the woods. But he fooled all the skeptics. It was the strict discipline that made this possible.

He was extremely farsighted. Once Mary and I were

walking across campus and he grabbed us—he was always grabbing someone—and took us to see the holes he had dug for the sewage disposal lakes, or lagoons. I said, "They look awfully big to me." And they weren't even full yet.

He said, "We need them big. No point in digging small ones. We'll be using them a long time, a hundred years from now, after I'm dead and gone. This place is going to keep on growing. Wait and see."

He knew the camp would still be around when he was gone. He could see things other people couldn't see, believe things no one else would believe. He never lost that faith in his dreams. There were many times when he must have been terribly discouraged. But he never showed it. He didn't hold grudges or carry his grief on his sleeve. This is a sign of a great man. He had nerve, he had guts.

He was everywhere. He was involved in everything, the sewage disposal, the administration, the music. He was a miracle man. However, I don't think he knew much about tuning pianos or singing. I challenged him once on a radio interview with four people from Interlochen. Dr. Maddy told a lot of anecdotes. The rest of us told about all the things he could do. Toward the end of the interview, I piped up, "There must be something you *can't* do. I'll bet you can't sing." With that, we got an instant quartet going and Dr. Maddy was singing. He wasn't much of a singer, but he made a racket.

He was always popping into classes to see how things were going. Sometimes he would just pop in and out; other times he would stay a little longer. He spent a great deal of time with the Junior Orchestra and Beginners' classes. He was especially interested in the younger kids and how they were progressing on their instruments.

During our first year at camp the students started calling me Uncle Ken, and I loved it. It was the best of all music to my ears. It drew us back to Interlochen year after year. After the Academy opened and Mary became head of the girls' dorm, we were Father Ken and Mother Mary. Isn't that ridiculous? By then our grandchildren were coming here.

We decided to sell our house in Detroit and make this our permanent home. We bought a cabin on the Boardman River that had belonged to the columnist Ann Landers and her husband, who was an avid trout fisherman and also very rich. It was only five miles from Interlochen.

When I called Ann Landers's husband about buying the house, he asked for some basic credentials—my job, income, terms of payment, and so on. When I told him I worked at Interlochen, he laughed a good-natured, hearty laugh, and said, "Well, I don't know whether you can afford it. I hear they don't pay people out there."

I assured him we were solvent, and we bought the house. Mary was a born-and-bred city girl, but she loves it. We have a trout stream in our front yard, a salt lick for the deer, cardinals to feed, no curtains on our windows, canoers going down the river, the gorgeous changing of seasons—and Interlochen.

It's true: no one comes here for the money. If you're coming here to get rich, forget it. I never made any money, but I believed in the place, I never thought it would fold. Mary and I both felt it was the place we had to be. Not many people would give up their homes and move up here just to teach at Interlochen. I'd scrub floors, I'd do anything, I'd even pay them to be here. That's what Interlochen does to you.

Once you are here and get the feel for it, you are never the same again. I still remember that wonderful silence we felt the first time we walked in the woods here, our feet cushioned in pine needles. You have to be an Interlochen person to appreciate it. You have to believe in it. And you have to believe in it for itself, the way Dr. Maddy did, instead of for you. He didn't want anything out of this personally. He did it for the kids and the music. That's why we're still here, to help him carry on what he started.

As this is written, UNCLE KEN, as the kids call him, is still carrying on as conductor of the major choral events at Interlochen and tying flies for trout fishing in the Boardman River that swirls around the sloping green of their lawn. Mary sings as the canoes float by.

29
A. CLYDE ROLLER

"There was a certain aura about him. When he was present, you knew that things were right."

🦋

My first summer at Interlochen was the worst year I ever spent in my life. We had sunshine only eighteen days in eight weeks. Our two young children developed chicken pox, and for four weeks my wife and I had to take turns caring for them, bringing trays of food that slopped over.

The University Orchestra, which I was hired to conduct, was a disappointment. There weren't enough players. We had to rehearse piecemeal.

We lived in a primitive cabin near a place called Slow Horse Crossing. It had high beamed ceilings and one twenty-five-watt bulb. The North Star put out more light than that bulb. The walls were gray and depressing. I was being paid peanuts. I thought, Why in the world did we leave Amarillo to come to this godforsaken place? We were crazy as bats!

But we met some interesting people. Dr. Maddy was marvelous. When we went back home, time began to erase the unpleasant things. We realized that if Interlochen was that bad every year, the place would have been closed down long ago.

One day my four-year-old son said to me, "Daddy, you know we're sure lucky." I asked, "Why?"

He said, "Because you and Mom took us to Interlochen, and we got to meet all those people, like Dr. Maddy and Dr. Hanson [Howard Hanson of Eastman] and Mr. Grainger." I nearly fell out of my seat. I was amazed that he even remembered their names. I got goose pimples.

The upshot, of course, was that we went back to Interlochen the next year and have been going every year since 1951, and all of those years have been just as marvelous as the first year was bad.

The place just grew on us. You didn't come here to make money. But meeting these people is something money can't buy. My kids practically grew up here. The values they learned here can't be put into words. Interlochen really changed the lives of my children. They both went into music and became members of the San Antonio Symphony. It changed my life, too, all our lives. I don't think anybody—no matter who it is—can come to Interlochen and not have his or her life dramatically changed. It's because of the spirit of the place and the values and philosophy of Dr. Maddy.

He was not only a dreamer but also a doer. We used to laughingly say, "Dr. Maddy is digging another hole." Which he always was. But if he was not digging a hole literally, he was digging a hole as far as his dream was concerned, and always implementing it with an energy that would finally blossom into a building or a policy or a new idea of some kind. He was always doing something for somebody. He had the humility to tell a student, "You come and talk with

152

me any time you want to, and if I can help you, I will."

Dr. Maddy really loved these kids. He always called them his kids. I was telling my students the other day what a great person he was and how he influenced all our lives, and if he were here now, he would really be rehearsing you hard and he'd be at you to do the right thing—but all the time he was doing this, he'd be loving you to pieces.

A case in point is the way he protected his students. He never wanted them to be embarrassed if they hit a sour note or something went wrong. Once I remember something went terribly wrong at a concert at the Bowl. They were playing the Tchaikovsky Sixth, which has a solo part for the bassoon. The bassoon player was about three notes into his solo when a key stuck. Or something. The bassoon squawked.

Dr. Maddy abruptly stopped the orchestra, turned to the audience, and said, "If you people are going to cough, it seems to me that you could do it in a much more quiet manner. You don't have to disrupt the concert. Please cough quietly."

The people in the audience sort of cleared their throats and coughed quietly, as if on cue, not realizing that the bassoon's squawk was anything but a cough.

A bassoon is a tricky instrument. A good bassoon player knows how to get a stuck key to come unstuck with some prying and tinkering. But it takes a little time.

There were more burps from the bassoon.

Dr. Maddy saw that his bassoon player needed more time, so he turned to the audience again, whipped a handkerchief out of his pocket, coughed into it, and said, "Now we're going to start again. If you need to cough, please cough into your handkerchief."

By this time the bassoon player had his key fixed, and the concert went on with his bassoon solo, which he played superbly. And I doubt if anyone realized he'd had a problem. Dr. Maddy's coughing act was a fine cover-up for what might have been an embarrassment to his bassoon player.

Dr. Maddy never walked adagio. He always walked presto, or allegro. Very rapidly, quickly. There was a certain aura about his presence. You knew that when he was there, things were right.

A. CLYDE ROLLER was one of Interlochen's most beloved conductors and Dr. Maddy's first choice to be his successor. He declined because he didn't care for administrative details. He wanted to be only a conductor. He still is guest conductor to prestigious orchestras all over the world, and he returns to Interlochen each summer as guest conductor of the World Youth Symphony Orchestra in benefit concerts with winners of the Van Cliburn competition.

30
WILLIAM REVELLI

"You start out believing and then do it. That was Joe."

&

I first came to Interlochen in 1929, the second year of camp. The place was quite primitive then. In fact, most of the faculty and staff lived in tents and cooked their own food, just like tourist campers, but only for a couple of years until things got going. They were paid a dollar a day.

I was lucky enough to be housed in the old Pennington Hotel during my first summer. Then my wife, Mary, and I were assigned to a rustic camp cabin. Very rustic. One night I heard something whooshing around the room. I pulled the string on the light, and Mary screamed, "Bill, it's a mouse that flies!"

It was a bat. That was the way things were in those early days. Like camping out.

I could see what Dr. Maddy was dreaming about. He was a very confident person. When he envisioned something, there was no such thing as no. He was a first-class optimist. This place would not have happened if it had not been for him. Once I overheard him and Mrs. Maddy talking about his idea of eventually turning it into a year-round school. Mrs. Maddy said something like, "If it happens . . ." Joe reminded her, "Never say *if*, say *when*."

He was about the only person around here who envisioned Interlochen in its entirety. Financial problems were the least of his worries. His main concerns were with the aesthetic, cultural, and educational aspects of his program.

I didn't come here for the money. Nobody did. Later, when I started coming as a guest conductor, I didn't get paid. There were many of us who came for a weekend of guest conducting. None of us were paid for that. I came because I felt there was a need for the type of thing Joe Maddy was doing, and I wanted to make a contribution to its development.

I shared Joe's belief that there is nothing in life richer or more rewarding than taking something from its birth and nurturing and developing it. It's the pioneer spirit. Joe Maddy was one of the great pioneers in music education, in Rochester, New York, and Richmond, Indiana. In my own way, I was a pioneer in Hobart, Indiana, at just about the time he was leaving Richmond.

I went to Hobart in 1925 as a teacher and supervisor of music. During my second week there, I went to the school superintendent and asked permission to organize an instrumental music department, because no one in the school played an instrument. He said, "I think it's a great idea, but I want you to know there's no room to rehearse in, no time schedule, and no budget."

So I borrowed a drum every morning from the local jazz drummer, got some students together to meet at seven o'clock in the morning, and we started a school band. That's known as pioneering. For many years I was director

156

of high-school bands and instrumental music in Hobart.

I think the reason Joe Maddy was able to draw so many band and orchestra conductors and teachers to Interlochen, men and women who were enthusiastic and dedicated leaders in the field of instrumental music at the time, was that they all wanted to contribute to the pioneering and development of the camp, its purpose, objectives, and ideals. They were willing to come here at great financial sacrifice. There was no thought of salary. When you're imbued with that pioneer spirit, your reward comes from accomplishment, not money.

I've been here almost every year since the camp was founded. My association with some of the great conductors has had an impact on my life and career. Howard Hanson, the famous conductor and composer from the Eastman School in Rochester, New York, was one of them. I always wondered how in the world Joe Maddy ever got Howard Hanson to come to Interlochen.

I think people underestimated Joe Maddy. He was a very astute person. He had kind of a dual personality. He never struck me as a salesman. He was very positive, never had negative thoughts. But he wasn't the strongest person- ality I'd ever known. In some ways he was almost demure. He wasn't aggressive, or overbearing, or pushy the way some salesmen are. He got what he needed another way. Some salesmen talk five minutes too much. Not Joe. He would give you the picture and let you take it from there. He didn't force himself on you.

When he talked about Interlochen and his plans for the future, I was never sure Joe could pull it off. Because to my mind he wasn't a salesman. He didn't match the proto- type.

But I was dead wrong. He was the greatest salesman on earth indirectly, because he believed in what he was doing. He didn't push you or wheedle you, but when he left you, he left you with complete belief in what he'd told you. I tried for years to understand it, and to this day I still don't understand. There was sort of a mystical quality about him that probably nobody can define.

Once when I was talking to Mr. Stone, I got bold enough to ask him why he had given so much money to Interlochen. He replied, "Because of Joe Maddy's belief and what he is doing for thousands of kids all over the world."

I can't think of anyone else who could have "sold" Mr. Stone, a super salesman in his own field, on such an ephemeral thing as Interlochen, except Joe Maddy.

His credo boiled down to two simple things: (1) *belief* in what you're doing, and (2) *faith* in carrying it through. You start out believing and then do it. That was Joe.

WILLIAM REVELLI still does guest conducting but is now retired and lives in Ann Arbor.

31
OSCAR ZIMMERMAN

*"The first thing it does for young musicians, it separates
the sheep from the goats."*

❧

My wife, Mary, sold me on Interlochen. She came here as a
violinist in 1931 and fell in love with the place and Dr.
Maddy. She came by bus from Colorado and stopped some-
place along the way to visit relatives. Her aunt slipped her
an extra ten-dollar bill for spending money. While she was
asleep on the bus somebody robbed her. When the bus left
her here she had no money.

She called the camp and asked for Dr. Maddy. He told
her to get a hotel room and take a nap, and he would drive
down to get her. At eleven o'clock at night, Dr. Maddy and
Mrs. Maddy and the band director all arrived at the hotel to
pick her up. Dr. Maddy paid her hotel bill. She was almost
seventeen.

"I just felt as though my father or someone had taken
care of me," she told me a couple of years later when we
were engaged to be married. I was professor of double bass
at the Eastman School of Music and principal bass in the
Rochester Philharmonic Orchestra. I met her in Ann Arbor,

Michigan, while I was on a vacation in 1932. I met Dr.
Maddy at about the same time.

A student of mine wanted to introduce me to Dr.
Maddy. I remember it vividly. We went to his home, and
behind his home he had a studio, and he was sitting there
at his desk with the score of the Sibelius First Symphony.
He began telling me right away that he was going to do
Sibelius up at Interlochen.

Interlochen? Sibelius at this little pipsqueak music
camp in the north woods? I thought the man was nuts. I
had just played that symphony in Philadelphia. No way
could it be played by a bunch of amateurs, kids. Sibelius
was still a little new in this country. Not too many had
heard of him yet. I was surprised that Dr. Maddy knew so
much about him and was so determined that his students
were going to learn.

We spent a very friendly hour or so discussing Sibelius,
and I went back to teaching. Then Mary told me about her
second summer here and her unforgettable impressions of
Howard Hanson as he played his *Romantic Symphony* for
the first time, on the piano, just for the students. They were
all sitting on the floor, around the stage, listening to him
play. He would play and then stop and explain something
to them. Everyone was mesmerized; there was absolute
silence. "I'll never forget it as long as I live," Mary said. "It
was one of the most exciting experiences of my life."

That was the summer that Howard Hanson dedicated
his *Romantic Symphony* to Interlochen, and the first time it
was ever played by an orchestra.

Howard Hanson's name helped Joe Maddy a lot in
building Interlochen. But it was really Dr. Maddy who did
it. He wasn't a sit-still visionary. He went out and made it

happen. He had tenacity, he was determined, and he knew how to separate the sheep from the goats.

Some students come here thinking they are wonderful, and they find out they're not quite so wonderful. It's more difficult than they anticipated. I think it helps them decide whether they are really serious about music or just music lovers. They have to learn self-discipline. They have to practice whether they feel like it or not. They must have the courage to go through those challenges even if it scares them to death.

With string-bass players I try to play down challenges as much as I can. The bass is a section where all the instruments play the same part. They're not soloists. I try to make the kids feel that, after all, they're here to learn the music and to be better bass players, and what difference does it make if they're first, third, or fourth? I tell them that maybe to be first flute is much more important than being first bass. You all play the same music and you are here to learn it, and it doesn't matter where you are playing it from, first, fourth, or tenth.

We were here in the very early years. It was nip and tuck whether we were going to get paid or not. Joe Maddy was a great music educator. But he was a dreamer, a visionary. If he had two million, he would spend three million, and he would always end up all right. I can't remember a time when he wasn't raising money. The Blanket fundraiser after concerts was one of them, when people threw coins into the blanket and there was always a little German band or something to attract them.

They even sold the tablecloths from the dining room at the end of one summer to raise money. That was when the old hotel was still run by Mr. Pennington and the faculty ate in the dining room, not in the line. You sat down with a tablecloth, silver, and goblet, and you were served. You were segregated from the students. Some of the college girls were earning their tuition by being waitresses. You had to be quiet. You couldn't be banging and talking and laughing because the hotel guests were there in the dining room across from where you were. But at the end of that summer they auctioned off the tablecloths, and now we go through the cafeteria line and eat on bare tables. It's better.

Our first son was born here. We call him our "Interlochen baby." Our two boys grew up here. They're now professional musicians, one a bass player in the Dallas Symphony, the other a trombone player and teacher.

Interlochen was a great influence on our lives. Dr. Maddy always treated campers like his own children. That's why he could build up a high-school orchestra that was absolutely the best in the country. He had such faith and optimism. And unquenchable enthusiasm. To him it was all important that this dream be realized, and I think there must be many men who would give their lives—or say they would—to achieve this. But Dr. Maddy *did*. That's the difference.

There was something about those eyes when he was telling you about something . . . you were sold.

Mary and I lived off campus in a rustic house with a telephone, one of the few. Often at night I would get a call from Dr. Maddy saying come over to his cottage. He wanted to play chamber music. He'd play viola himself. He loved to play. We would play from ten o'clock at night till three in the morning. He could whack off anything on the viola. He wasn't a virtuoso violist, but he could really plow through those parts. He knew them. Extremely well. He usually

162

called me when he wanted to play a piece with a bass part. Sometimes he would pick the Schubert Quintet in C Major, which had two cellos, and I would play the second cello part on the bass.

Mrs. Maddy always stayed up all during these chamber music sessions and served cake and coffee.

Joe Maddy was like a juggler juggling fifty things at once. I was always amazed that he knew so much about this area. He knew it like the back of his hand. He knew everything about the lake, where the best fishing was, where the currents were, the prevailing winds, and where to go if a storm hit. He got a frantic call one night from visitors whose two kids (not campers) had been down at the beach. A storm had blown up and they had been gone a very long time. Dr. Maddy said, "Don't worry. I know just where they are." He did. He drove right down and picked them up. He knew in this storm exactly where on the beach they would be. As Mary always said, "I'd trust my life with him."

OSCAR ZIMMERMAN was one of the country's leading double-bass players. He was a professor of music at the Eastman School of Music in Rochester, New York, and a member of the Rochester Philharmonic and the Philadelphia Orchestra. He also played in the NBC Symphony under Toscanini. He taught at the National Music Camp from 1934 to 1938 and left when Petrillo banned union musicians from the grounds. When he and his wife returned each summer to their cottage near the camp, they spent each Sunday evening standing just outside the camp grounds listening to the concerts. (They weren't allowed inside even to listen!) Zimmerman returned as a faculty

163

member in 1944, after the Petrillo ban was lifted. He died in 1987, but during his lifetime he wrote twenty-six books for double-bass students. The books, largely excerpts from orchestral literature especially adapted for double-bass players, are still very much in demand. His family carries on the business, Zimmerman Productions.

32
FREDERICK FENNELL

"I really came alive down there on the Bowl stage. As far
as I am concerned, life dates from then."

❧

I first heard about Interlochen in the summer of 1930, and
my life has never been the same since. I was listening to a
radio broadcast at my home in Cleveland and an announcer
came on and said, "This is music from Interlochen. . . ."

The announcer painted word pictures of the place, the
wonderful lakes, the woods, the land of the gently lapping
waters and the beautiful towering pines. . . . He made it
sound like the elysian fields. I saw castles come up in the
sky in front of me. In those days on radio you made your
own pictures, not like television today.

The way the announcer described the place in a few
words was marvelous. But it wasn't the place, the camp, the
woods that made the castles in the sky. It was the music
coming from high-school kids, the way they played—that's
what knocked me out. I had to be where that kind of music
was being played. I didn't know how I was going to get
there, but somehow I would.

The music was Howard Hanson's *Romantic Symphony,*

conducted by a man named Dr. Joseph E. Maddy. It was the first time I'd ever heard of Howard Hanson, the *Romantic Symphony*, or Joe Maddy. But the memory of it is as vivid and poignant today as it was sixty years ago.

I was a percussion player in our high-school band and orchestra. I asked our music director about Interlochen, and he gave me a little booklet about it. I memorized it. I knew everything about the place before I came. I applied for a scholarship and got it because they needed another good percussion player.

I thought I was pretty good until I got here and found that there were four other percussion players infinitely better than I was. But I learned from them. They were part of my education. I learned by listening, I learned by watching, and I learned by competing against them. That was true from the beginning of camp.

Interlochen makes an achiever out of you. It makes you want to achieve because those around you have achieved and are making it and so can you.

I knew from the time of my first rehearsal in the Interlochen Bowl that this was the place I had to be for the rest of my life. I was just seventeen. Somehow I got the feeling that previously in those seventeen years I had just existed, but that I really came to life down there in the Bowl. As far as I am concerned, life dates from that.

I was a high-school camper here three years, from 1931 to 1933. Then I went to Eastman to study with Howard Hanson and came back here on the faculty and then as a guest conductor, and I've been here ever since.

It was Joe Maddy who steered the course for me. The first summer he said, "Now Freddy, you're going to be here for three summers. But you're not just coming to camp. You have to set yourself a goal each summer. Learn something new."

So the first summer I worked at perfecting my percussion—I was up against some tough competition—and the next summer I learned how to be a twirling drum major, and the third summer I concentrated on composition and conducting.

I did the drum majoring only because I wanted to go back and be a drum major in my high-school band. But that's what got me into Eastman, I know. I really worked at it. In those days Dr. Maddy was the conductor for six of the eight weeks. The other two weeks we had guest conductors, and Howard Hanson was one of them. Everyone was in awe of him and everyone wanted to play in his orchestra, but he didn't need many percussion players for his *Romantic Symphony*. And I wasn't the best. We drew lots to determine who would be in his orchestra that week. I didn't win, but my best buddy percussionist did. He agreed to swap weeks with me so I could play with Dr. Hanson and talk to him about going to Eastman. Somehow it worked.

Ever since I could remember, I had wanted to be a conductor. I took conducting classes at Interlochen under Vladimir Bakaleinikoff, a viola teacher and a superb conductor. But in those days you didn't even think about being a conductor until you were sixty or seventy years old.

As a young kid after getting out of Interlochen, the only way to be a conductor was to find something to conduct that nobody else was interested in. I found that out at the Eastman School of Music with the school's first band. Nobody was interested in having a band there, no one was interested in conducting one, nobody took anything like that seriously—so they let me get away with it. I started as a conductor because I was willing to work with a kind of "underprivileged" musical ensemble.

Of course it was different at Interlochen. And the difference was Joe Maddy. There were many who helped him along the way, but it was always a one-man operation. He's the man who dug the holes, cut the stencils, took care of all the details, and delegated authority to a lot of other people to make them feel important, but he's the one who went out drumming up business and money.

I'm sure there are many music educators who have dreamed big dreams and wished they could do what he did, but he had his dreams and then got out of bed and went out and did something about them.

He had those unknown powers of faith and positive thinking. To him nothing was impossible. He had a knack for making others feel the same way.

This camp does not exist for the faculty, the staff, the board of trustees, or even for its many friends. It was started for young people who wanted to play music together. Dr. Maddy always started on the premise that the kids could play. And they could do a different concert every week for eight weeks whether they thought they could do it or not. At that time there was no place doing things like this. A lot of music educators thought he was crazy. But the kids didn't. They would rehearse all week on a piece they'd never heard of before, and by Sunday night's concert time they had it all pulled together.

One of his great appeals was the music he chose to play. Most of the kids had never played such music in their hometown bands and orchestras.

He knew such a great deal of music and he knew every note of it by memory. One of the things that always surprised the kids and everyone who watched him conduct was that he could whistle his way through any piece of music he conducted. That's what he used to do if anything went wrong in a rehearsal. Many times when we were not familiar with the music, we'd fumble and stumble and lose our way in the score, not able to follow the conductor. We might be completely lost, but he never lost the composer. He would go right on whistling until we all fell back in somehow. He was a great whistler.

I still remember our first rehearsal of the 1933 camp season. We were doing Beethoven's *Eroica Symphony*, many of us for the first time. He had whistled us about halfway through it when a sudden thunderstorm hit and cloudbursts of rain started pouring in on the stage. The stage crew quickly pulled the curtain to the center of the Bowl. It's the only time I ever saw it pulled except for operettas. The *Eroica* isn't the quietest piece of music in the world anyway, even under ideal circumstances and acoustics. On an outdoor stage, and behind a closed curtain being battered by rain, it sounded almost deafening, especially toward the end, which builds up to a grand finale of roaring kettledrums and a big series of crashing chords with cymbals.

I was doing my bit with the kettledrums when Dr. Maddy's dog, a big German shepherd who had been lying quietly and attentively throughout the rehearsal, leaped up and let out a series of howls through those crashing chords. He couldn't take the noise any longer.

He was as good at howling as Dr. Maddy was at whistling. He howled his way all through the final chords of the symphony, drowning out not only the music but the thunderstorm as well. I never heard anything like it.

During my three years as a camper, one of my biggest thrills was playing the Blanket after concerts to try to get people to drop in a little money. At that time I don't think anyone knew where the next can of beans was coming from. It was very touch and go. Students were willing to do anything that could help. John Minnema, the Blanket man, was a great spieler, as we called him. At every afternoon and evening concert, he would begin by welcoming the audience to this beautiful place and would then remind them that this cost a lot of money and would they please drop some money in the blanket as they departed.

We all contributed by doing our own Blanket thing after the concerts, anything to get people's attention, stop them from just leaving, and get them to throw in a few coins. Anything we could bring in was welcome. We had little brass bands, cowboy music, student combos of all kinds. I played solos on the vibraphone, an instrument resembling the marimba. It always drew a lot of attention.

In all the years I knew Joe Maddy, he was always trying to figure out ways to raise money to keep his camp going. And he did a pretty good job of it. Anyone else would have given up after day one. He was full of today but really more full of tomorrow, always thinking ahead, planning for a future that nobody in the world believed would ever happen except Joe Maddy.

He never conned anyone into anything. He just sweet-talked them. That isn't the same as conning. If he hadn't sweet-talked people, I don't think there would have been a second summer or even a camp to begin with. He sweet-talked some of the finest music educators and conductors to come here for peanuts. They were paid a dime and a

170

button to work their heads off for these kids. Why did they do it? For the same reason Joe did. Kids turned them on.

After I came back here on the faculty, we became quite good friends. I was never in awe of him, but I had great admiration and respect for him. He had to sweet-talk me into calling him Joe instead of Dr. Maddy, which I finally did, with reluctance. He never did like being called *Doctor* Maddy, though most people called him that.

I think my turning point came when he sweet-talked me into riding with him into Traverse City. It was a harrowing experience. I'm an out-and-out blowhard for Joe Maddy. The only bad thing I can say about him is that his driving skills didn't match his musical talent. He had the car radio on, a tape recorder going, was making notes with one hand, driving with the other, talking incessantly, and going ninety miles an hour down a two-lane highway. It was the most frightening experience of my life. He was a madman behind the wheel.

But he was unique. When I was with him I always felt that I was in the presence of a man who didn't have enough time to get done half the things he wanted to do in one day, or a month, or a year . . . a man who made all kinds of impossible things happen, a man who was driven solely because he had something truly extraordinarily wonderful to live for. Not many people attain that in a lifetime.

The camp rules were always explicitly laid down on opening night. Anyone who did not wish to follow them could leave then. Joe Maddy and T. P. Giddings were right from the beginning. They knew that talent without discipline is the greatest waste in the world. Their discipline started with the uniform that put everybody on the same level, rich or poor. A kid from the sticks had the same chance as the one from a Texas ranch. I had never met a kid from Texas or Oklahoma or California. Neither had most of the others. We quickly learned that we all put on our corduroy pants the same way and that the rules were not rules in the usual ordinary sense but simply guidelines to make it easier for us to accomplish what we were there to do—to make music. Things get done at Interlochen better than anyplace else because of this discipline.

I knew when I came here that first summer that music was something I simply could not live without. All the people I met here, all the music I heard here, I can't imagine life without it.

Dr. Maddy used to talk to me a lot about what he thought was important for the students to carry away from here, and that was the spirit of the place—not only a search for one's own excellence but the greater message of music that comes from having been together with fellow young people. There is a kind of spirit that has always been here that started with Joe Maddy and was kept alive by Joe Maddy and is still here.

So much is different now. The camp has grown enormously. It is a small city all by itself. Campers today have a different approach to things, a different outlook, a different language, but the spirit of the place, I think, remains exactly the same. People frequently ask me, "Hasn't it changed a lot?" I don't think so, and I hope it never will.

Dr. Maddy once gave me an autographed picture of himself on which he wrote, "To Freddy Fennell, a living example of the spirit of Interlochen."

172

I still treasure that picture. If I am a part of the spirit of Interlochen, that is great with me. I would be very happy if that was so. I do think there is such a spirit. I hope that every kid who comes here has some way of catching some of it.

FREDERICK FENNELL is still a conductor at Interlochen.

33
HENRY CHARLES SMITH

"He knew everything that everybody did, every move we made, and he talked constantly about his dream for a great arts center."

🌿

I first came to Interlochen in the summer of 1948. I couldn't afford it. I pumped gas, worked as a typist, and put money away for three summers during high school to get here. I had just graduated and was about to turn seventeen when I came, from a suburb of Philadelphia. I'd heard about Interlochen. Some of my classmates had been there.

When I arrived, it was everything I had expected and more. I was overwhelmed by the excellence of the group, the music they played, the forest, and Dr. Maddy's total, dedicated involvement. Even as a camper, I felt, correctly, that he knew everything that I and everybody else did. And when I came on the faculty I knew that he knew every move I made. He came and played viola at all of my rehearsals.

I was here as a student only one year, then on the stage crew for two years, then trombone teacher and conductor of the University Orchestra and band. Meanwhile, I won the national auditions against sixty other trombonists for a job in the Philadelphia Orchestra under Eugene Ormandy, one of the twentieth century's greatest conductors. I was only twenty-three, and suddenly I was solo trombonist with the Philadelphia Orchestra, one of the best symphonies anywhere.

I vividly remember one of my first concerts. The guest artist was to be a violinist doing the Brahms Concerto in D Major. We had rehearsed it. He had to cancel due to illness. Two hours before the concert, the program was changed.

The Brahms Second Symphony was substituted for the concerto—and with no time for rehearsal. The other players knew it. Mr. Ormandy figured I didn't since I was new. He came up to me and rather apologetically said he was sorry to toss this one at me without a rehearsal.

I told him not to worry. I had played it at Interlochen. He said, "Interlochen? Hmmmm."

Some years later, in 1964, Eugene Ormandy and the Philadelphia Orchestra spent a week in residence at Interlochen working with the students, doing rehearsals and four concerts.

I became conductor of Interlochen's World Youth Symphony Orchestra in 1981. One of the most delightful guest performers I've worked with—and they're not all that easy—is Itzhak Perlman, the great violinist who is unique in the rarefied ranks of superstar artists. But he's like a big kid. He loves to have fun—he's a horrendous punster, and he likes to play games with and tricks on the kids. Once when we were rehearsing the Tchaikovsky Concerto in the summer of 1990, the first cellist began lagging a little. He turned to her, winked, and said, "Chicken!" That churned her up.

I have conducted for Perlman many times in different

places. Usually a guest artist chooses the piece he or she wants to perform or submits a list to the conductor, and we make the decision together. For his 1991 concert at Interlochen, Perlman gave me a list and just said, "Take your pick." We had already done the Tchaikovsky and Mozart concertos for his guest appearances the two previous summers. So this time I chose the Max Bruch Concerto No. 1 in G Minor, not only because it was in the big four of major violin concertos but because we had a huge number of violin players in the orchestra and I already had them studying it.

It was a very difficult and demanding piece, as every concerto is, especially for teenage musicians. Every concerto is a show-off for the player and his instrument. That's why we have weekly concerto auditions at Interlochen, and concerto winners are looked on with pride and admiration by their colleagues and teachers. It's a great honor to be a concerto winner. I suppose it's a little like being an Oscar winner in Hollywood. We schedule many concerts during the season especially to show off our concerto winners, and these are always well attended by the other students. The concerto auditions have been an Interlochen tradition ever since Dr. Maddy started them, and we had many concerto winners or runners-up when Itzhak Perlman arrived for the rehearsal for his concert.

I had confidence in our orchestra. Still, the Bruch Concerto is a real challenge for the best players in any orchestra. I expected a few instructions from Mr. Perlman. He came on stage only a few minutes before rehearsal time. We greeted each other, and I asked, "Do you have any instructions? What do you want to tell me? What do I need to know?"

"Well, it's a great piece you've picked," he said. "Let's go." So we started the rehearsal.

He is so sure of himself. He instills confidence in the players. The next night, for him our World Youth Symphony Orchestra played the Bruch Concerto as well as seasoned professionals.

The sellout audience gave him continuing clapping-and-shouting standing ovations. He graciously came out for four encores. Then he shook hands with the concertmistress and congratulated the orchestra. "You're terrific, you're wonderful," he said with fervor. "You must be the best of Joe Maddy's dream. You're the best student musicians I've ever heard. But I hear you've got a wonderful deal here, something that turns you on and makes you play music like that." He paused, wiped his brow, and added, "I'm sure glad I didn't arrive here on Bloody Friday. I'd probably never make it through those challenges."

That nearly brought down the house with laughter.

Bloody Friday is the day set aside for sectional tryouts and challenges, when any student can challenge any other player in the section and try to win his or her chair by playing better.

During his concert, many eyes were focused not only on Perlman but on the little sixteen-year-old concertmistress who handed him his violin. She had survived many Bloody Fridays to retain her position as first-chair violinist. She was also a concerto winner.

Her name is Carmen Rosu-Nicolescu. She was a defector from Romania. She arrived at Interlochen—I don't know how—and announced at the end of her first summer here, 1990, that she wasn't going back to Romania. Everyone gulped. A number of camp people debated about taking

177

her home with them and helping her. She has been unofficially "adopted" by an Interlochen couple, now living in Minneapolis. They have fed and clothed her, given her medical attention, bought her a new violin, and treated her like a daughter while the rest of her family is still in refugee status in Germany. Both of her parents are musicians. Her father is a trumpeter, her mother is a pianist, and two younger children are also musicians.

Some of us have tried to figure out a way to bring Carmen's family to this country. If Dr. Maddy were still alive, he would find a way. He could always find a way to do what needed to be done.

One summer when Van Cliburn was here for a benefit concert, Dr. Maddy noticed that Van seemed a little worried about something. And indeed he was. He had accepted an engagement with the Philadelphia Orchestra for the following week, doing Tchaikovsky's *Romeo and Juliet*, both playing *and* conducting.

"I don't know why I agreed to do it," he said. "I don't know how to conduct."

"Don't worry about a thing," Dr. Maddy said. "We'll go find Henry Smith. He knows the Philadelphia Orchestra and he's a conductor—we'll teach you."

Van was leaving in a few hours. We had no time to waste. It was a very hot August afternoon, 110 degrees in the shade, and absolutely sweltering inside the only empty practice cabin we could find in which to give Van Cliburn his first and only conducting lesson. We got the *Romeo and Juliet* score from the music library. We had done the piece with our orchestra only the week before. Van of course could probably play the piano part in his sleep. Joe Maddy and I gave him the score and had him conduct *Romeo and*

Juliet—without an orchestra—from beginning to end, again and again, until he knew how to do it. It was sort of a collective conducting lesson.

Dr. Maddy would whistle the parts—he was a fantastic whistler—and I would sing or hum or da-da through them while we turned and swung and pointed and gyrated for all the instrument sections of an imaginary orchestra. We must have been a spectacle to watch.

We soon had an audience. Word spread that Van Cliburn was in the practice cabin, with no piano, and strange antics were going on. The campers trooped down and stood outside looking in the windows, sometimes squealing and laughing. In that heat! Today's kids would call it "cool"—the thrill of watching their favorite performer in anything.

We spent two hours taking Van Cliburn through his conducting lesson for the *Romeo and Juliet* with the Philadelphia Orchestra. He was, as usual, a huge success. But it didn't take him long to give up conducting.

HENRY CHARLES SMITH, as solo trombonist with the Philadelphia Orchestra, played more than two thousand concerts with Eugene Ormandy and other of the twentieth century's greatest conductors. He has been on the faculties of the Curtis Institute of Music and other leading music colleges and guest conductor of some of the country's major symphonies. He currently divides his time between Interlochen and Arizona State University, where he conducts the orchestra and teaches conducting at the doctoral level.

34
HELEN OSTERLIN
*"He had this goal, and nothing was going
to get in the way."*

❧

I first met Dr. Maddy in Ann Arbor. My husband, Dr. Mark Osterlin, was a pediatrician and medical director of the Children's Clinic at the university. Joe talked him into coming to Interlochen to be the camp's medical director. That was in the summer of 1931. Mark was the only doctor. The hospital was very small but adequate. There weren't many students here then.

I was involved with the arts. So I took voice and other classes at Interlochen every summer and sometimes helped out in the camp office. After Mark died, I took his place on the board of trustees, and I've been here ever since. Sixty years . . . that's a long time. We built a house in Traverse City, out on the peninsula, where the Grand Traverse Bay sunsets are beautiful and it's only twenty minutes or so from Interlochen. Less if you're riding with Joe Maddy.

Through the years, I have probably attended more concerts and board meetings than anyone else but Joe Maddy. I have had the rare privilege of watching his dream

180

grow almost from its beginning. I have seen its impact on this community, the whole surrounding area, and the world beyond.

Joe Maddy was a man of great enthusiasm. He inspired and generated it in others. He really bubbled over. His vision was tremendous. He could really see into the future.

I recall the time he wanted to purchase some land and his board at that time refused him. As it turned out, that land today is worth hundreds of thousands of dollars. If they had listened to Joe, they would have made a lot of money. He had the capacity to see things others couldn't.

No one ever thought it would be possible to pay for some of the holes he dug. My husband, Mark, was with Roger Jacobi once when Joe was digging the second hole for Kresge Auditorium, enlarging it with no money. Mark just stood there with his hands on his hips and said, "Jesus, how does that man do it?" Somehow or other he went out and got the money from somebody in order to finish the job.

It must have been that special charm he had. He could win anyone over with that infectious laugh and a smile.

He really didn't have the qualities of a salesman. For one thing he spoke too fast. One time he was firing off a bunch of instructions for things he wanted me to do. I said to him, "Joe, would you please slow down—I can't keep up with you." His thoughts were ahead of his speech. He was really ahead of most people in his thinking. But we wouldn't be where we are today if he didn't have that capability.

I saw Joe frustrated and discouraged many times, but he didn't stay that way very long. He usually tried to find a solution to it. He was a real fighter. He fought against a jet base being built, and a prison camp, too. He did this for the good of the area as well as the good of the camp. There was a reason for everything he did.

He had an unbelievable ability to concentrate. I must say, I was never too comfortable riding in the car with him. He was always looking around and jotting things down with one hand and driving with the other, talking and flinging his arms around. It was scary.

Joe loved to show people around the camp. If they were the least bit interested he would show them every part of it. Even the lagoon and the plumbing system that were put in.

He had many interests. One was religion. He read a great many books on various religions. He also was into buying surplus supplies. He always knew where he could use things. If it was a bargain he'd buy it. Not just one, but a dozen if they had it.

His spirit is everywhere at Interlochen. It's as if he is looking in on everything. He may not like what he sees sometimes, but he is there. I can actually see Joe looking down over the Bowl and saying, "This is great. It is going on just as I hoped it would."

HELEN OSTERLIN, who now lives in Traverse City, remains one of Interlochen's strongest supporters. She is an active member of its board of trustees.

35
GEORGE WILSON

"You're vice president, aren't you?
Just go ahead and do it."

❧

I remember arriving at Interlochen in the summer of 1929, with cinders flying in the windows of the train. I thought we'd never get there.

I was a senior at the University of Illinois, played in the college band and orchestra, and I had already decided on music as a career. I was a violinist and a student conductor of a high-school orchestra in Champaign. But I didn't come here as a musician. I came as a librarian, to help get the camp's music library organized and under way. I was working in the university's huge band library, at that time a mecca for the college band business, and one day a man named Joe Maddy came in. The next thing I knew, I was on my way to Interlochen. It was very new then, only a year old, and I didn't know much about it, but I thought, well, anyway, it sounds like a nice summer job.

I quickly learned that the librarian's job entailed a good many other things I knew nothing about, including being a handyman for the stage crew. One time all the lights went off on the stage just before a concert and it was my responsibility to get them turned back on. I didn't know how. Dr. Maddy was getting all set up to conduct the orchestra.

When he realized we were having problems with the lights, he bounced backstage, fussed around with the plugs and switches, and got the lights back on—all without a single mutter of complaint to any of us who were working on them.

That was one of my first impressions of Joe Maddy. Here was a man who was in charge of the whole place, yet he was willing to take the time to help us work out a problem. The man was always busy. I never saw him when he wasn't bouncing on or off the stage, in and out of the library, everywhere. But he was never too busy to help us when we needed it.

The other thing that impressed me very much was the kind of music these kids were playing here. I came from a good college orchestra. But I was totally floored when I heard the Tchaikovsky and Brahms and other symphonies being performed so well by students on the high-school level. They were doing more here in eight weeks than they would in nine months in a university music program. It really inspired me to have a bigger vision of my own goals. I knew I would come back.

I spent two summers here as a librarian, then got my master's degree and a teaching job, and came back in 1945 on the faculty, and with a wife and family. We enrolled our daughters in camp and settled in—for a long stay.

In 1957 Dr. Maddy announced that he wanted me as vice president. By that time I had a full professorship at the

University of Illinois. Being vice president of Interlochen meant a full-time, year-round job.

I knew I could stay at Illinois with financial security and know where I was going. At Interlochen you're not sure what's around the corner. There are always financial problems. But it was a challenge I accepted. My wife, Mary Alice, was a little upset because I was going without a contract. I have never signed a contract in my life and never expect to. I doubt if Dr. Maddy ever asked anyone to sign a contract. You just took his word and went along with him and hoped for the best.

He was vague in outlining job descriptions. I really didn't know what was required of me as vice president. Soon after I arrived in my new position, I asked him just what he wanted me to *do*? What was my job?

He said, "You're vice president, aren't you? Just go ahead and do it."

He never gave anybody instructions. I didn't have any specific duties. I didn't even have an office. I worked in a corner of his office for years. I was just vice president. What do vice presidents do? Get busy and do it, whatever needs to be done.

So one of the first things I did was to ask him about the enrollment files. I couldn't find any. He reached in his pocket and pulled out sheets of paper, crumpled and folded to about an inch thick, and said, "Now this one is the orchestra, this is the band, these are the violins . . . cellos, trumpets, string bass . . . ," and so on.

He had a bunch of marks, numbers 1, 2, 3, 4, 5, all in colors, red or blue. The red was for former students, the blue for the new ones. He knew exactly how many students he had enrolled in his orchestra and band for that summer and what instruments they played. But nobody else knew. He didn't have the names, but he had his band and orchestra players all figured out by instruments and jotted down on that wad of paper in his pocket.

My first mission, I decided, was to try to bring some order out of all this chaos. So I developed an enrollment procedure and a flat file that we could open up and understand, with the students' names, instruments, and other relevant information. But Dr. Maddy still always kept his own file in his pocket.

The financial problems continued. Often our records were so far behind, we didn't know where we stood. Many times Mackmiller would tell us not to cash our checks for about five days because there wasn't enough money in the bank yet.

But somehow Dr. Maddy always got us through it. I believe his success was built on three basic ingredients: discipline, competition, and spiritual underpinnings. These are essential to character building, and Dr. Maddy's dream for Interlochen was not only to inspire young people in music and the arts but to also help shape and mold them for life, with or without music. He achieved this through:

- *Discipline.* This starts with the uniform and the admonishment, "Stick to the rules, please. If you don't like them, go home." There was never any compromise. Students who broke the rules were sent home. Discipline is essential for success in any field. It was imperative for Interlochen, a summer music camp for boys and girls. T. P. Giddings was a first-class disciplinarian.
- *Competition . . . challenges.* The Bloody Friday challenges are a vital part of our program. They give children the

186

motivation to go as far and as fast as they can. The competition helps prepare them for life. Because life is competition. When you get out of here, you have to meet challenges.

- *Spiritual underpinnings.* Interlochen is not known as a religious place, and Dr. Maddy was not known as a religious leader; yet there has always seemed to be a strong pervasion of religion throughout Interlochen, and I think it's part of his philosophy of character building. Character building was very important to him, and Mr. Stone speaks of it in very strong terms. We believe the spiritual underpinning in the lives of people is extremely vital. There are many who felt that Joe Maddy preached his own religion and had only one god—Interlochen.

He wasn't outwardly religious—he wasn't a religious fanatic—but I believe he was a deeply religious man. He was a very moral person and he demanded high standards and moral principles from everyone, especially young people. He knew and taught and inspired the values that are important in building character for anything worthwhile in life, not only music. In fact, I believe it was Joe Maddy's deep faith in Interlochen that created the real aura of spirituality that has always been here.

Through the years, many students and visitors have told us, "This isn't only a musical experience; it's a religious experience."

Dr. Maddy was a dreamer, a genius, an educator, and a fine musician. He was way ahead of his time, a giant in the early music-education movement. There was no ceiling on his dreams, no way to keep up with him. I tried. We all did.

JOE MADDY OF INTERLOCHEN

We sometimes tried to tell him to take it a little slower, a little easier. It was no use.

The most frightening part of my job as vice president was being obliged sometimes to ride in the car with the president. It was dangerous. He always had that ubiquitous pad and pencil for jotting down notes while driving. That was how he kept track of his ideas. I refused to ride with him in later years.

GEORGE WILSON is now retired and lives in Traverse City.

36
ROGER E. JACOBI

"It wasn't easy following in the footsteps of a legend."

The first time Mary Jane and I came up here, we were on our honeymoon. We had been married just a week. I was teaching music in Ann Arbor—the same system Dr. Maddy was using there in 1924. I came here to help improve the band program. That was the summer of 1948.

Word got around that we were newlyweds. Some of the youngsters in the band decided to get out their horns and serenade us, marching around our cabin at three o'clock in the morning. When we started to walk into the dining hall later in the morning, there was Dr. Maddy pointing his finger to the exit sign. But we walked in and nobody said a word, and we all sat there spilling our cereal because we were shaking so much. The kids had really been noisy. I figured it would blow the lid off my camp job. But we never heard a single word about the whole thing.

I came back in 1953 as program director with Mary Jane and a baby only ten weeks old. It was an extremely hot day—impossible. In those days we had to boil the baby's formula, which we did in Ann Arbor and packed it all up to bring to Interlochen. Minerva Turner put the bottles in the camp's kitchen refrigerator. After that we kept them in a big refrigerator on the porch of our cabin.

There was a huge motor on top of the refrigerator, and every time that thing would go off, the whole house would shake. The refrigerator was a relic, probably resurrected from Henry Ford's peace ship, and put on our porch because we were the only ones with a baby. The refrigerator rarely worked. It always went off when Mary Jane was trying to cool the baby's formula, and she would be standing there with tears pouring down her face while the baby was screaming.

Mary Jane didn't care much for our living arrangements. We were on the second floor of a two-story cabin, with four families sharing one bathroom. When the alarms went off in the morning, everybody ran like mad to get there first. And then there were all the mice we heard and saw at night, running up and down the walls.

This wasn't Utopia. But little did we dream then that one day we would be living at Norpines, the president's home.

In 1971 I accepted, with some trepidation, the trustees' decision to appoint me as president of the Interlochen Arts Center, after a few other interim directors had tried and didn't make it. It wasn't easy following in the footsteps of a legend. No one could match his fire and brimstone.

It took me several weeks to make a decision. I had just been appointed dean of music at the University of Michigan. That's a pretty good job to leave. I sat down and methodically wrote out pages of notes—reasons why I should take the job and reasons why I should not take the job. The list for why I should not take the job was about a foot and a half long compared with the list of why I should take the job, which was about an inch or two long.

I took the job anyway, for two reasons: (1) I loved Interlochen; and (2) I believed Joe Maddy was a genius who left a legacy so precious and fragile that it should never be lost. I wanted to help continue his dream.

When I was a staff member, I discovered he was a man of many creative ideas. He would dream up more ideas in five minutes than ten men could in a hundred years. Not all of his ideas were practical, but if he thought up one hundred ideas, at least ten would be good ones. A lot of people thought he just had the ideas and left it to others to carry them out. This is not true. He could delegate authority very well, but he could also design anything and follow through on the details if he wanted to. He was very practical, tangible. His eternal optimism was what made this place a success. He didn't know the meaning of the words *no*, *can't*, or *impossible*. They didn't exist in his vocabulary.

The character building of the young people here was very important to Dr. Maddy. He always felt that if the standards were kept high, Interlochen would have no worries in the future. He wasn't like a horse with blinders though; he was willing to change. He always tried to get from one point to another in the shortest time possible. If he found resistance, he would make a ninety-degree turn and try something else. But he never lost sight of the goal. That was the key.

Sometimes the staff people were dubious and maybe

too critical about some of the crazy ideas he had up his sleeve. We didn't want to do what we thought was stupid or dumb. So we would walk outside and to the center of the campus and make a 360-degree turn and take a long look at everything around us. It made us realize this man did all of this; that he couldn't be all wrong. Then we'd go in and get back to work.

Dr. Maddy was really pushing for the winter school then. I can't name one person on the staff who supported him in this. I think I was the only one who supported him, and I did this for a reason. I thought the man was a genius.

Everyone warned me, "Don't ever ride with Joe Maddy. He'll scare you to death." I rode with him on many trips. I was never fearful. He was a very good driver; otherwise I wouldn't be here now to tell about it. We had some close calls, but the Lord always took care of him. When I rode with him, I always used it as an opportunity to learn more about Interlochen. I soon learned that he talked in direct ratio to his driving. Or vice versa.

I once asked him about his problems with [James C.] Petrillo, the music union czar who caused so much trouble for Interlochen. When he first started talking, we were going only seventy miles an hour. He became more and more agitated. By the time he finished it was ninety miles an hour.

The only time I ever saw him slow down was when we hit a sandbar and got stuck. We were in the middle of nowhere. He said, "Dagummit, I'm never coming this way again." But he was prepared. He knew exactly what to do. We got out of the car and he said, "I have these booster springs. Now, all you have to do is jack the car up and put these frames in between the body of the car and the frame underneath, while I go out and find some boards to stick under the tires."

So I was under the car thinking, What if the jacks don't hold? He came back with two big boards and a big smile on his face and said, "These will get us out of here." He got in the car and gunned the engine while I pushed the back, trying to stay out of the way of those boards. If the tires really grabbed them, they would shoot out the back like bullets. We got out of the sandbar okay. That was the kind of charmed life Joe Maddy led. He might find himself in a pickle, but the Lord always had a way out for him.

One problem we had with him: Joe Maddy didn't always talk in complete sentences. He was always thinking ahead of where his mouth was. You'd be following him, listening to his words, and all of a sudden you could be looking him in the eye and not have the slightest idea of what he was talking about. That's because in his mind he had changed subjects and hadn't bothered to tell you. You thought, "What in the world is he talking about now?" It was a struggle to follow him. Then he would give you a key word and you'd think, "Ah-ha! Now I know what he was talking about." This was the way his mind worked, always thinking about ten things at a time.

He was a man of great vision. When I became president, my vision was dollar signs. Money to keep Joe Maddy's dream alive. I had no expertise in fund-raising, but I learned that it is an integral part of a president's job, so I did it. Just as Joe Maddy would have expected me to.

Mary Jane was my greatest asset. We worked as a team.

She was the hardest-working unpaid employee we ever had.

ROGER E. JACOBI retired as president of Interlochen in 1989, after eighteen years as Joe Maddy's successor. He and his wife, Mary Jane, have remained active in promoting the cultural growth of Interlochen.

37
MARY JANE JACOBI
"It wasn't easy, but I did it."

৵

As the president's wife and therefore official hostess of visiting VIPs, I had to learn to adjust.

It wasn't easy, but I did it.

I usually wore the camp uniform—knickers. But on some occasions I felt it was more appropriate, as wife of the president, to wear a skirt. In July 1975, President Gerald Ford and Mrs. Ford paid us a visit. An advance team had been dispatched from the White House to get everything set up. They installed a White House hot line in the Stone Student Center. Security guards were everywhere. It was an awesome sight to see two armed men up on top of Kresge Auditorium.

And I must have been an awesome sight to a lovely young woman in the advance team who came up to me and said, "Now, Mrs. Jacobi, what will you be wearing that day?"

I was wearing my blue corduroy skirt and blouse and navy-blue hose—camp uniform. I said to the young woman, who was very chicly dressed, "Well, I'll be wearing a blue blouse just like this one, and I'll be wearing a blue skirt and blue hose just like what I have on. In other words, I will look exactly the same except it will all be nice and fresh and clean." She got the message. There would be no change even for the president of the United States.

When the Fords arrived, Roger had charge of President Ford while I escorted Mrs. Ford around the campus. I took her over to the dance building, where arrangements had been made for the dancers to do some demonstrations for her because of her interest in dance. Then I took her to a little scenic spot behind the Bowl, where a cabin group of high-school girls waited to greet her with a surprise gift. The route had been predetermined. I knew about the surprise.

With appropriate pomp and circumstance, they presented a pair of blue corduroy knickers to Mrs. Ford. She was delighted.

We had an afternoon concert by the High School Symphonic Band and Choir, with George Wilson conducting. After the concert, President Ford thanked us with a glowing tribute:

> President Jacobi and all the people connected with Interlochen, let me thank all of you on behalf of Betty and myself. I don't know who made the list of selections, but everything that was on the list was on my own list of favorites. May I congratulate the superb young people in the band and chorus. It makes all of us extremely proud to see young people with such enthusiasm and talent and dedication. As I sat back there I couldn't help but be impressed with the words that are

on the back of the stage, "Dedicated to the promotion of world friendship through the universal language of the arts." That is a hallmark and something all of us should strive for and seek. All of you who participate make a giant contribution to a better world. Thank you very much.

We said good-bye to President and Mrs. Ford, and as we were leaving we turned around, and here all of a sudden were Mr. and Mrs. Stone, their daughter, Donna, and their son, Clement and his wife, Barbara. They had all come up for the concert because of Mr. Stone's connection with the president. It was a last-minute decision. They hadn't wanted to bother us at this busy time so they hadn't called; they just came.

Jessie hugged me and said, "I'm hungry."

We hadn't made any arrangements for food. We didn't keep a lot of food in our house because we ate most of our meals at school. We said, "All right," then drove over to our house at Norpines and went through the kitchen cupboards. We found a jar of peanut butter and some jam. Mr. Stone stood at the end of our kitchen counter making peanut butter-and-jelly sandwiches, and we dined on them at our own little yellow table in the corner of our kitchen-dinette.

It was the first but not the last time we had our "yellow table" snacks. The Stones seemed to like our little yellow table. One time Roger picked them up at the airport and brought them home. We had invited some other people. There were about a dozen of us sitting glued to the television news coming out of Washington. Our TV was in the corner of the dinette. I fixed some cheese and crackers.

When the news was over, Mr. Stone went into the kitchen and fixed himself a peanut-butter-and-jelly sandwich.

I was impressed. Here was a man, one of the great philanthropists of the world, who could be dining at any restaurant, and here he was at our house eating peanut-butter-and-jelly sandwiches.

He also liked ice cream and cherry pie. He invited his friend Bob Hope to come and give a benefit concert at Interlochen. We went with the Stones to meet Bob and Dolores Hope at the airport. It was cherry season. The orchards were loaded with ripe, red cherries, and Bob wanted to stop and get some. He ate cherries and was throwing pits out the window all the way back to camp.

When we got there, Mr. Stone said, "Come on, Bob, you have to have your ice cream." Mr. Stone always liked the ice-cream cones from our Melody Freeze. He took Bob over there, and Bob dutifully ate the ice cream—on top of all those cherries.

That evening we had a reception for them in our home. Somewhere in the middle of it, we realized that both Bob Hope and Mr. Stone were conspicuously missing. We found them in the kitchen with our student helpers, laughing and joking and eating cherry pie.

I later learned that Mr. Stone, in addition to his other talents, has some interesting culinary skills. At his home, on the cook's day off, he substitutes as chef with his favorite menu—sauerkraut and a scoop of cottage cheese topped with strawberry preserves.

My job as wife of Interlochen's president, and official hostess for visiting VIPs wasn't easy but no worthwhile job ever is. Certainly it was never dull. And the wonderful friends we made, like Jessie and Clement Stone, made it infinitely rewarding.

MARY JANE AND ROGER JACOBI divide their time between their summer cottage at Fife Lake, near Interlochen, and a winter home in Palm Beach, Florida. Their hobbies are fishing, sailing, and playing piano and trumpet duets together.

"What is life but a series of preludes?"

Joe Maddy

Part IV
Les Preludes

On May 4, 1991, W. Clement Stone celebrated his eighty-ninth birthday. He and Jessie were the first ones on the dance floor and the last to leave. They had quite a few grandchildren to dance with.

On August 4, 1991, exactly three months later, Clement Stone was at Interlochen listening to tributes to Dr. Maddy. This was a "Centennial Summer" celebrating the hundredth birthday of Dr. Maddy.

When the Sunday morning convocation and tributes were finished, Mr. Stone presented the new president with a $100,000 check, a challenge grant that had been met.

It was the same month thirty years before that Mr. Stone met Joe Maddy and began giving millions to help Dr. Maddy achieve his goals.

38
CENTENNIAL TRIBUTES TO
DR. MADDY

⚜

HELEN OSTERLIN

I am honored to be a part of this celebration of the hundreth anniversary of the birth of my friend Joe Maddy.

My association goes back a long way. My love for Interlochen began when my husband, Dr. Mark Osterlin, came here in the thirties from the pediatrics department of University Hospital in Ann Arbor to take care of the medical needs of the Music Camp. The small hospital was located in the High School Boys' Camp.

It is impossible for me to tell you what Interlochen has meant to my life and to many others'. In fact I would not be standing here today had it not been for the National Music Camp and Joseph Maddy. Interlochen has been a great part of my life since that time.

There were many difficulties in the early days. Lack of money was a great problem, as was acceptance by the public at large. This was a new venture in our area—a summer music camp situated in a wooded area near Interlochen.

But Joe Maddy attracted supporters too numerous to name, and he drew an outstanding faculty and many worldfamous guest artists over the years.

I know so many of you understand what I am talking about when I say "the Interlochen spirit," and my hope is that we never lose it. This is a very special place. It is the talented and dedicated youth and faculty who make this institution what it is. There is magic in the air with all these young people making beautiful music and engaged in all the arts.

Joe Maddy instituted so many ideas that were ahead of his time. He loved young people and had faith in their potential. The system of challenges was one of his great educational concepts.

On the original blueprint of Interlochen there was a "radio room." Little did anyone know that by 1963 Interlochen would be operating its own noncommercial radio station. Today that station is WIAA and WIZY, and it has just finished a successful campaign for listener-supported funds amounting to $210,000.

The year 1962 was a very special year. The National Music Camp High School Orchestra performed on the White House lawn for President Kennedy. And Joseph Maddy opened the Interlochen Arts Academy in the fall of 1962. The Academy would not have been possible without the magnificent support of W. Clement Stone.

Composer Percy Grainger made this statement when he was at Interlochen: "Your idea of the National Music Camp is a perfect idea, perfectly in harmony with the nature of music itself, perfectly adapted to the national life of America today, perfectly carried out. Its conception and execution are both equally inspiring."

We are honoring a great leader, and it has been my privilege to have been a small part of Interlochen and a friend of Joe Maddy.

ROGER E. JACOBI

I assume that nearly everyone at this Interlochen service believes in some sort of supernatural being. If you believe in God as I do, then perhaps you also believe that some people are placed on earth to achieve great things. These people seem to have an extra God-given gift which makes them unique and enables them to have a tremendous impact on the people of the world.

I believe that Joseph E. Maddy was one of them, because of the influence he had on music education around the world, and because of the great impact he had on the lives of countless people, both children and adults.

In the summer of 1928, the National High School Orchestra Camp was born. And even though the nation soon suffered its greatest depression ever, the camp survived because the *idea* was sound, the students were eager, and the faculty and staff were dedicated to this new concept of music education. It also survived because the people of Interlochen and Traverse City, as well as others across the land, joyfully came to help the man and his dream of a music camp.

Someone once said, "Joe Maddy's last name predicted his life's work." Let's examine each letter of that name:

204

M—is for Music

A—is for Art

D—is for Dance

D—is for Drama

Y—is for Youth

That is how Joseph Maddy dedicated his life.

He traveled the country far and wide, conducting every student band and orchestra he could find, because he knew that by doing so he could recruit outstanding students for his camp.

Joe Maddy had a special "believability" about him that made people want to help him. I remember well the years when he was developing his ideas for a year-round arts academy.

Many said it couldn't be done. Then Dr. Maddy met W. Clement Stone, who believed in Maddy's dreams and wanted to help him. With the generosity of Mr. Stone and others, winterized buildings were built and the Interlochen Arts Academy opened its doors in 1962, when Dr. Maddy was seventy-one years old.

Although he lived to see only four years of the Academy, its future was secure for the first ten years because Mr. Stone simply picked up the deficit, giving Interlochen time to reorganize and become self-supporting after Dr. Maddy's death in 1966.

I want to say a few words about what Dr. Maddy did *beyond* the formation of this institution—things which, indeed, made him a giant in music education. Listen to just a partial list of his many achievements that had an impact on the nation:

- He developed the first complete symphony orchestra in any American school (Richmond, Indiana, 1920).
- He conceived and developed the first practical system for teaching all instruments of the band and orchestra together at the same time (1922).
- He became known as "the father of instrumental music education in the American schools" because of his teaching system.
- He wrote countless musical arrangements of the classics for school bands and orchestras—where none existed before—thus enabling them to perform great music on their level.
- He conceived, organized, and conducted the National High School Orchestra, 1926 through 1930, to demonstrate to the nation's developing instrumental-music educators what talented, gifted, and creative young people could accomplish when properly motivated.
- He convinced the School Administrators of America in 1927 to urge all schools to include music and art as major subjects with schooltime classes and school credit.
- He originated a system for teaching instrumental music by *radio*, which was carried coast to coast by NBC from 1936 to 1939.
- He initiated the Michigan Youth Arts Festival in 1963 to recognize and demonstrate the growth and development of young people in *all* the arts in Michigan.

Although Joseph Maddy received countless honors and awards, such as seven honorary doctoral degrees and the Horatio Alger Award, his greatest love was Interlochen and the students who, as he would say, came to camp "to test their talents with others" and "to do more in less time."

He knew they would not all be future artists. But he did know that when they left Interlochen they would leave with something special. They would learn the joy of succeeding by working hard. They would learn what it means to live, share, and grow together. They would develop new friendships which would last a lifetime. And, for most, the times spent at Interlochen would be the happiest and most productive times in their lives.

Yes, we are celebrating the centennial year of Joseph Maddy's birth. But we should also recognize that 1991 is the twenty-fifth anniversary of his death. And still, his dream continues today as if he were still alive. Those of us who work for Interlochen today are *caretakers* of his dream.

I wish you would do me a favor when you leave the service this morning. Locate your favorite spot on campus. Then take a moment and *slowly* turn around 360 degrees and look at Joe Maddy's living dream. You'll find it wherever you look.

He hasn't been here to see it in twenty-five years, but his presence is still felt everywhere because of the goodness and the soundness of the dream he had for Interlochen and the talented youth of the world.

And that's the challenge to those of us who have the opportunity to follow in the footsteps of Dr. Maddy—to keep his dream alive at Interlochen, namely, the development of youthful artistic talent. In doing so, we must be respectful of the past, live in the present, and look to the future.

Yes, Joseph E. Maddy was a man born for greatness.

RONALD F. STOWE

One of the most subtle, and yet profound, signatures of Joe Maddy on the legacy of Interlochen is the ritual of *Les Preludes*. The spectacle, the music, the dance, and the explosion of emotions which take place on that last Sunday night of camp reflect far more than the majesty of the composition or the skill of the performers. They become a permanent reminder of the uniqueness of Interlochen, of what happened to our lives, and more specifically to our values, while we were here.

That the centerpiece of the final ceremony should be *Les Preludes* is no accident. The poignant message that the culmination of our experience here really is a slingshot into the rest of our lives is fully appreciated only after we have returned to our homes, our schools, or our jobs. And that was exactly what Joe Maddy had in mind.

You have heard a great deal about the history of Interlochen under Joe Maddy. . . . But I would like to talk about another side of that remarkable man—the man who thought constantly in terms of new beginnings. It is especially from this aspect of Joe Maddy that we can learn lessons of importance to our lives today.

Joe Maddy never looked back; indeed, he was obsessed with the future. He had so many ambitions, so many goals, that his aspirations seemed to outrace time; he wanted to move faster and to accomplish more than the clock and the calendar would allow. Many of you may be surprised to learn that before he died Dr. Maddy obtained a charter for opening a college at Interlochen, a dream that seems futuristic even now.

Perhaps most important of all was the fact that his

ambitions were profoundly based on the belief that the arts would give a depth of meaning and common understanding to people's lives unmatched by virtually any other experience. "Dedicated to the promotion of world friendship through the universal language of the arts" was no empty phrase then and is no empty phrase now. There really is a common bond among us all, regardless of our particular heritage, and the arts allow us to sense a deeper meaning for our existence, to reach deeper into our souls.

This belief in the value of the arts was coupled by a then-radical but now commonly accepted conviction that the arts could and should be shared by everyone, not just the elite, the wealthy, or the powerful in our society.

Joe Maddy played a creative, constructive, and insistent role in bringing musical instruments, training, and performance opportunities into the public schools and hence into the daily lives of millions of average Americans. His obsession with generating dollars for scholarships to Interlochen translated itself into life-shaping experiences for thousands of students who are now major contributing members of our society.

We would miss the best of Joe Maddy if we think of him just as history. He was, in fact, a rebel, an innovator, a breaker of tradition and china and glass. He bulldozed through the legions of it-can't-be-doners; he abandoned old expectations; he truly was a revolutionary in educator's clothing.

But he got away with it because he was in touch with fundamental values of human nature. Although he certainly did not run Interlochen as a democracy in terms of governance, there was nothing more important to him than the equality of opportunity and the recognition of real

accomplishment. Talent was always highly valued and re-
vered, but talent unapplied left him cold.

He knew as well that no one man or even a few together could accomplish what he had in mind. To reach
young students from all parts of this country he needed a
faculty and staff which possessed both the highest skills
and the greatest personal dedication; the highest skills
because the talent of tomorrow's leaders is so extraordinary and demanding, and personal dedication because the
Herculean efforts required to build and preserve this institution go far beyond the normal business call of duty. One
thing is certain: realizing the potential of Interlochen is no
nine-to-five job.

As a former camper and student at the Academy, I was
the direct beneficiary of both the skills and the caring of
this wonderful community, and I am extremely pleased
that this summer both of my children are campers here. I
could not wish for them a more wonderful experience.

To help young students realize their extraordinary
potential requires an extremely unusual combination of
artistic creativity, hard business judgment, and a genuine
sense of common purpose. These values remain essential
today if we are to preserve Interlochen and adapt it for the
future.

We must modernize or perish. We must be hard-nosed
and progressive in our decisions. We are not isolated from
the rest of our society, and it is often a harsh and competitive world out there. Sometimes that calls for evolution;
sometimes it demands more radical steps. Joe Maddy certainly used both.

But in either case, whether we move quickly or slowly,
we must remain constant with our fundamental values, and

we must bring about those changes through full utilization and cooperation of the Interlochen faculty, staff, alumni, trustees, friends, and supporters.

We are all here in the presence of something greater than ourselves. It is our duty, and our goal, to sustain and nurture it into the future. Just as Joe Maddy propelled us into the rest of our lives through the ceremony of *Les Preludes*, let us use this celebration of the hundredth anniversary of his birth to renew our commitment to the values which make this institution great, to do whatever is necessary to meet the rapidly changing demands of the future, and to do so together, taking both strength and inspiration from our past. I believe Joe Maddy would approve.

39
THE DREAM LIVES ON

⚘

Would Joe Maddy approve?

In the summer of 1991 there was an air of uneasiness about the "new kids on the block," new administrators trying to build a "corporate image" with only dollar signs in their eyes. Students now had to pay to go to concerts, even to audition for concertos. Uniforms were optional; most wore knickers, but many did not. There were brand-new big signs posted along the highway entrance to Interlochen that sent shock waves through many who were familiar with Interlochen tradition.

The signs had oak leaves on them! Someone had neglected to tell the corporate image makers that Interlochen's symbol was the pine tree, not the oak. John Philip Sousa had dedicated his "Northern Pines March" to Interlochen. Every summer for years students had sung the camp-opening theme song, "Sound the Call." It's very first words are, "Sound the call to dear old Interlochen, land of the stately pines."

For many who loved Interlochen and all it stood for, the violation of the pine-tree symbol was sacrilegious— almost as bad as the desecration of the American flag.

And fifteen dollars just to *audition* for the honors concertos? "Budget cutbacks," said the bean counters over parents' protests. Dr. Maddy would roll over in his grave and spew fumes of wrath at anybody charging his kids for concerto auditions.

The Blanket days were long gone. There was a pop-corn and ice-cream stand in its place. Instead of tossing in coins, people from the surrounding area were paying top prices to see and hear Las Vegas–type entertainers.

There was more emphasis on pop concerts, less on student performances. Many visitors were taken aback by the new look of the place. Some thought it looked more like a shopping mall than an educational institution. Students were calling it Disneylochen.

There was an undercurrent of grumbling and some troubling questions. Were they trying to make rock music into an art form or turn Interlochen into a pop festival?

As one student put it, "I'm a musician. I came here to study music, to learn something that contributes to my education in the arts. My grandmother loves Julio Iglesias, but I'd rather hear a student recital. However, I realize we need revenue."

And the pop concerts were bringing in big revenue.

For eighteen years Interlochen had been guided by the strong leadership of Roger Jacobi, who knew and worked with Joe Maddy and carried on his basic philosophy and traditions. He had succeeded in bringing financial stability to Interlochen without sacrificing its ideals, artistic integrity, or mission.

The new president, Dean Boal, didn't know Dr. Maddy, had never met him, but he seemed assured that Joe Maddy's mission was being carried out and would continue to be.

"There is always a transition period of adjustment when a new administration takes over," he said. "There is always some resistance to new ideas and change. Our mission is just as clear today as it was back in 1928. Joe Maddy would be the first to recognize the need for change. He was a revolutionary in bringing new ideas and changes in music education.

"Audiences today are growing up on television and computers. Young people take these things for granted. Our students need to live in a world that includes computerization and computer imaging, which is now part of the art world. We have to evolve to a point where our classes are concerned with living in a world that reflects changes in the arts."

Many feel that Interlochen is too precious and fragile to let it evolve into a world of "computer imaging" and that it will survive the onslaught of television and computers because its caretakers, the board of trustees, do care about and understand the meaning of Joe Maddy's dreams. This was made clear in a Memorial Tribute to Dr. Joseph E. Maddy on July 29, 1966, by the board of trustees:

> . . . To all of us who must carry on the great work and process he started, he also left a monumental challenge: first to understand the real meaning and intent of his dreams and his goals and, second, to consummate the material plans by which he sought to achieve his aims. Through our devoted and dedicated efforts to

complete his dreams, we can hope to gain increased insight into the world of creative vision and imagination, which now appears to have been the fountain from which the magic of Dr. Maddy's genius poured forth. This is our obligation; this is our privilege; this is our goal.

Today the board of trustees remains as dedicated, as vigorous, and vigilant as ever, perhaps more so. Many of its forty members are former Interlochen students or parents of students. And though he has stepped aside as board chairman, W. Clement Stone still attends board meetings and keeps a guardian angel's watchful eye over Joe Maddy's dream.

So there are changes, but some things remain the same—the stunning beauty of the music from Itzhak Perlman's violin with the World Youth Symphony Orchestra, the soul-stirring marches of John Philip Sousa in the Interlochen Bowl with the Interlochen Sousa Band, the tears streaming down the cheeks of kids playing their hearts out at their farewell *Les Preludes*. . . . Can computers do that?

At times like this, there is a pervasive reassurance that Joe Maddy's spirit still lives and that his dream will endure in spite of the bean counters.

He was never looking for the pot of gold at the end of the rainbow. He already had it. He walked the rainbow. He reached the stars on wings of magic. Along the way he touched many lives and left a legacy to the world.

About the Author

❧

Norma Lee Browning is a former *Chicago Tribune* reporter and syndicated Hollywood columnist. She is the author of several books, including a biography of Joe Maddy and *The Psychic World of Peter Hurkos*. She coauthored *The Other Side of the Mind* with W. Clement Stone and *He Saw a Hummingbird* with her husband, Russell Ogg. She and her husband were associated with the National Music Camp for many years and were charter members of the faculty of the Interlochen Arts Academy when it opened in 1962. They were also a well-known photojournalist team who covered assignments all over the world until Ogg's death in November 1990. He took most of the photos for this book.